waiting *with* Gabriel

AMY KUEBELBECK

4/29/14

To Sarah,
Warmest wishes to you and to
the families in your care.

Amy Kuebelbeck

a story of cherishing a baby's brief life

LOYOLA PRESS.
A JESUIT MINISTRY
Chicago

LOYOLA PRESS.
A JESUIT MINISTRY

3441 N. Ashland Avenue
Chicago, Illinois 60657
(800) 621 1008
www.loyolapress.com

Cover and interior design by Eva Vincze

This book was typeset in Mrs. Eaves.

Paperback ISBN-13: 978-0-8294-2856-8
         ISBN-10: 0-8294-2856-9

Library of Congress Cataloging-in-Publication Data
Kuebelbeck, Amy, 1964–
  Waiting with Gabriel : a story of cherishing a baby's brief life / Amy
Kuebelbeck.
        p. cm.
Includes bibliographical references.
  ISBN-13: 978-0-8294-1603-9; ISBN-10: 0-8294-1603-X
  1. Grief. 2. Bereavement—Psychological aspects. 3. Infants
(Newborn)—Death—Psychological aspects. 4. Infants—Death—
Psychological aspects. 5. Loss (Psychology). I. Title.
  BF575 .G7 K83 2002
  155.9'37—dc21
                                        2002008555

Printed in the United States
10 11 12 13 14 Versa 10 9 8 7 6 5 4 3 2

For Gabriel

and for all other babies
whose parents' hearts
have been broken

contents

Chapter I

the  news

"You have a beautiful baby," the ultrasound technician said quietly. She was studying the flickering images on her screen, staring intently at the shadows of the tiny heart. I think she had already seen that our baby was going to die.

Outside, a cold April rain dripped onto buds waiting to bloom. Inside the darkened hospital exam room, the technician guided the transmitter over my five-and-a-half-months-pregnant belly, interpreting the sound waves that bounced back from our squirming baby. Legs, arms, brain, spine, kidneys—everything perfect. You know we're here to see the heart, right? we asked. Yes, she did.

Ultrasound exams have become almost a modern ritual of welcoming for expectant parents. No matter how many children you already have, that first look is breathtaking. There's a *person* in there! Fingers, a tiny mouth, feet, knees. Sometimes stretching lazily, sometimes rolling over purposefully, some times sucking a thumb. Most parents leave with a grainy black-and-white snapshot of a profile of a little face, a cherished image to be displayed on a refrigerator or in an office and later pasted on the first page of a baby book.

Ultrasounds are so routine that it's easy for parents to suppress the knowledge that the purpose of the exam is not to give them a sneak peek at their unborn child. The Kleenex in the exam rooms is not only for tears of joy.

At our first ultrasound exam at twenty weeks, my husband, Mark, and I brought our four-year-old and two-year-old daughters to see the new baby on "TV." The technician said our baby looked terrific and very active—so active, in fact, that she couldn't get a clear look at the heart. She said not to worry, so we didn't. We were so unconcerned that I went to a follow-up at the clinic four weeks later without Mark, bringing only our girls and some Tootsie Pops to keep them occupied.

"They sent you back just for the heart?" the same technician asked. "I won't even charge you for this one." But this time, she looked, and looked, and pressed on my belly harder to look some more. The Tootsie Pops were long gone, wrappers crumpled on the floor, fingers sticky, patience unraveling. She called a doctor in for yet another look. The doctor recommended a Level II ultrasound, a more detailed exam using more sophisticated equipment, "just to be sure."

So there we were at the hospital, an agonizing week later, trying to believe that the doctor had only ordered this exam for liability reasons. How relieved we would be to hear that the baby's heart was fine, to go home and call everybody with the good news, to say that the only detail we didn't know was whether we were having a boy or a girl. Mark and I had decided not to learn the baby's gender before birth, saving it for a happy surprise. We wanted to know only if that remote, unthinkable possibility came true, if something was terribly wrong.

The technician finally got around to studying the heart. The rhythmic whooshing seemed to fill the room, a reassuring sound in any other circumstances. She fell silent. Looking, pressing on my belly to try to nudge the baby into another position, tapping keys on the machine's keyboard. Looking. Was that the sound of my baby's heart or mine?

Finally, I ventured, "For telling our families—does it look like something is wrong?"

She kept her eyes on the screen and said quietly, "Yes."

People often use physical terms to try to describe what it feels like to hear devastating news—that it's like being punched in the stomach, like being hit by a truck, or like the world is crashing in on them. To me it felt like falling backward, as though the tiled concrete floor, the clay underground, all the subterranean layers of rock were simply and soundlessly parting to let me through to some other dimension. I think I might have actually fallen if it wasn't for that paper-covered steel examining table holding me up at just the right height to turn my head and bury my face in Mark's warm sweater.

I remember her saying the phrase "hypoplastic left heart syndrome," which Mark doesn't remember hearing at all that first day. From somewhere in my memory, I retrieved a medical phrase I never imagined I'd use and asked, "Is it incompatible with life?" She paused and answered, "I'll let the doctor answer that."

Clutching wet Kleenex and each other, Mark and I waited in the darkened room while the technician left to get a perinatologist, a specialist in high-risk pregnancies. The perinatologist came in and matter-of-factly explained that the left side of our baby's heart had not developed properly and that the condition was incurable and fatal. *Fatal. Our baby.* She said the pregnancy likely would continue normally and the baby would be fine until he or she was born, probably around the due date. Once the baby was born, we would have three options. We could try an aggressive series of three open-heart surgeries, beginning with a procedure called the Norwood, which would not be a cure but could possibly keep our baby alive indefinitely. We could try a heart transplant, but the odds of finding an infant donor in time would be low. Or we could provide comfort care, keeping the baby comfortable until death came naturally, probably within four to seven days.

Choked by tears, we asked if our baby would die peacefully if we decided on comfort care. She said yes.

The doctor recommended an amniocentesis to learn if the baby had any other problems. In an amniocentesis, the doctor inserts a hollow needle through the mother's abdomen to withdraw a small amount of amniotic fluid. The fluid is then sent to a lab, where it is examined for chromosomal information. How strange that when your mind is reeling, you hardly even care when somebody pushes a sickeningly long needle into your stomach.

We had one more question, the question we did not want to ask. Was our baby a boy or a girl? The

5

amnio results we would receive in a week or so would tell us for sure, but the ultrasound technician said she thought the baby looked like a boy.

She gave us a printout, an otherworldly profile of his little face.

I carefully tucked it into my purse so it wouldn't get wet in the rain.

ↄ

How surreal ordinary things seem after getting terrible news. Climbing into the car, paying the parking-lot attendant, waiting at a stoplight while hearing the rhythmic whooshing of the windshield wipers sliding the raindrops aside.

Back at home, I brushed past the babysitter and headed straight for our girls. I needed to hold a child of mine in my arms, even if it wasn't our new baby. The girls were only four and two, but they could tell something was wrong. Mark came in and we all sat on the couch together, Mark holding Elena, and Maria sharing my lap with the baby, who was kicking contentedly inside of me.

"The baby has a sick heart," Mark began, before starting to cry.

ↄ

Time is strangely suspended when you have awful news but haven't shared it yet. The telephone suddenly seems ominous; there is no good way to intrude into your friends' and families' daily routines to tell them that they're about to be plunged along with you into a different world.

Our phone rang first. It was one of my five sisters, Stacy, pregnant with her first child and due just six weeks after me. She knew we had been at the hospital and was calling to hear the news, hoping it was good. I only remember sobbing, "The baby has half a heart." Then I dialed my parents' number. My dad answered, and I told him the same thing, and that we thought the baby was a boy. Dad's mother had died just two weeks earlier, and now it looked as though his grandson was going to die too.

When my mom came home a short while later from running errands, she found him sitting in his favorite chair, crying.

~

That afternoon, the girls sat drawing at the dining-room table, one of their favorite pastimes. As she had been doing for months, Elena drew a stick-figure drawing of our family: Mark, me, and three progressively smaller children—herself, Maria, and the new baby. Her drawing was especially neat that day. I remember glancing at it and thinking, *Maybe we'll need that for the baby's funeral.*

I put on my raincoat and went outside to try to wrest last summer's dead Siberian irises from the earth, my tears and sweat mingling with the rain.

 ❧

Surprisingly, one of the reactions we didn't have was denial. Denial is, of course, the first of five stages of grief as classified and popularized by Elisabeth Kübler-Ross in her 1969 classic, *On Death and Dying.*[1] Once we got the diagnosis, neither one of us thought that the doctors must have made some mistake.

There was more of a sense of: *So that's what it is.*

Maybe our denial came earlier. Many first-time parents fret over every detail of pregnancy but are much more relaxed during subsequent pregnancies. For us, it was the reverse. My first two pregnancies were for the most part joyous and carefree. Morning sickness was minor, and I basked in the newness and richness of the experience. I looked forward to wearing maternity clothes, and sometimes I'd have to stifle a smile while covering hearings at the state capitol when one of my girls would nearly kick my reporter's notebook off my belly.

This time, our excitement was occasionally tinged with foreboding. I had never so much as called a nurse or my nurse-midwives with questions during either of my previous pregnancies, but for this one I called several times to ease my unfounded concerns. I worried that my morning sickness was really listeriosis, a type of food poisoning that can cause miscarriage or still-birth (and happened to be in the news that week). I even abruptly left work one afternoon to drive myself to the clinic, bypassing my nurse-midwives to see an obstetrician I'd never met before. (That particular worry also turned out to be nothing.)

And I vividly remember attending a Christmas concert by the Dale Warland Singers, a nationally acclaimed a cappella choir, at our neighborhood church. For an encore, the choir reverently walked back into the dimly lit sanctuary and began to sing "Silent Night." The arrangement was bittersweet, its cascading dissonances resolving gently. The voices were hushed, pure, achingly beautiful. Exquisite choral music has often transported me and sometimes moved me to tears. But this was different. I was so overcome not just by emotion but also by grief that I was afraid I was going to break down into great gasping sobs and ruin the moment for everybody in the packed church.

"I'm just so sad. I don't know why," I kept repeating to Mark as we walked home under the stars on

that clear, frigid Minnesota winter night. If anything, I should have been exhilarated. We had two
happy, healthy children, we were blessed with family
and friends, we both had jobs we enjoyed, and we
had just moved into a 1920s bungalow that I had
been enamored with since the moment I stepped
into its sun porch. And we were thrilled with our
still-private news that we were six weeks pregnant
with our third child, whose tiny heart was at that
moment beating, growing, forming.

Sleep in heavenly peace.

Perhaps on some level I already knew.

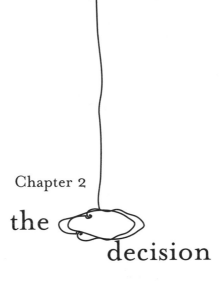

Chapter 2
the decision

Two of the most primal parental instincts are to keep your child alive and to protect your child from unnecessary pain. Those instincts usually do not collide.

With our baby, they did.

When modern medicine can offer even the remotest hope of a cure, the decision to try seems easy. Suddenly things that once seemed so terrible—the machines, the cutting through bone and flesh, even the experimental treatments—appear to offer a potential, though terrifying, lifeline up from the abyss. But what do you do when none of the options offer hope of reasonable success?

As we listened on that first awful day to the peri-natologist describe the possible surgeries, both Mark and I felt instinctively that we didn't want to put our baby through that magnitude of physi-cal pain and uncertainty. (I blurted to the peri-natologist at one point, "We weren't even going to circumcise him!") We could barely put it into coherent words to each other, but both of us felt a visceral need to protect our baby. Maybe protect-ing this child would not mean the usual tasks of getting vaccinations, putting safety plugs in elec-trical outlets, and installing gates on stairways. Maybe protecting this baby would mean keeping medicine at bay.

Of course, we didn't know enough yet to make an informed decision, so that became our imme-diate task. Before going to bed that first night, we logged on to the Internet to search for this topic that we'd never heard of and that was about to change our lives. Staring at the screen, my hand resting protectively over our growing baby, we saw the words *uniformly fatal.*

Later that night, we tried to sleep, the words *Norwood* and *transplant* and *uniformly fatal* pulsing through our minds.

❧

At least we had a reason to get up the next morning, for an even more detailed cardiac ultrasound with a pediatric cardiologist. Again we found ourselves in a darkened exam room, this time for several hours and in an area of the hospital dedicated to cardiac care. Whenever the door to our room opened, letting in harsh fluorescent light, I could see a white dry-erase board hanging on a wall outside the exam room that listed the day's appointments and the patients' ages and diagnoses. It listed mostly older people, but there were a few infants too. What were their lives like? My name was there as well, along with "fetal echo, HLHS." How strange to be associated with a medical condition.

The pediatric cardiologist was gentle but straightforward and not at all condescending. After the exam, we went to a small office, where he sketched our baby's heart with a black marker on a piece of scratch paper and explained generally what the reconstructive surgeries would attempt to do.

The goal of the surgeries is to rearrange the heart's plumbing so that the right side of the heart pumps blood to all parts of the body, doing the work of a whole heart. This refashioning cannot be done all at once because an infant's heart is so small and other systems are too immature, so it is performed as a series of three extremely high-risk open-heart surgeries.

The doctor also discussed with us the possibility of a heart transplant, noting that the odds of finding a donor heart in time would be poor.

And he said that given the enormous difficulties involved in either the Norwood or a transplant, comfort care was certainly still an option.

During one of our two lengthy visits with him that week, we asked him the question that probably no doctor wants to hear but is impossible for parents not to ask: What would you do if this were your baby?

He said carefully, "I've seen a lot of babies suffer unnecessarily."

He explained that even babies who survive one or more of the reconstructive surgeries face a real risk of grave complications, including strokes and brain damage from the lack of oxygen. They will never have normal circulation. Even more so than other "heart babies," babies with hypoplastic left heart syndrome (HLHS) almost always have problems eating and gaining weight, and many need to be fed through tubes that are snaked up their noses or surgically implanted in their abdomens. Some need pacemakers, and others eventually need a transplant anyway, rocketing them into another world of uncertainty.

The doctor also mentioned that his wife was a pediatric intensivist, a specialist whose lifework was treating critically ill children. Unlike us, she would not be queasy about surgery or feeding tubes or machines. She would have an acute sense of the miracles medicine could effect—and also of its limits. He said that after watching so many babies struggle in vain against HLHS, she felt strongly that she would not intervene.

In the weeks and months to come, we would think of that answer again and again. But not to intervene! That would mean standing by helplessly while our baby died. No parent should have to face such a chilling, hopeless "option." How would our baby die? Would he gasp for breath? Would he die in his sleep? Would he suffer?

Would he be scared?

Would we?

The cardiologist said that if we chose comfort care, death would probably come peacefully and that medications could be used to ease any discomfort. He told us that if we wanted to bring our baby home to die, hospice care would be a wonderful help, especially as death neared.

I needed to know another fundamental thing. I had been looking forward so much to nursing this new baby. Both of our girls nursed until they were a year old, and I cherished the shared experience. To be needed on so basic a level by a baby is such sweet intimacy, a sort of biological pas de deux in which a mother's body responds instinctively to her infant's needs. And every woman who's ever nursed recognizes the physical sensations that connect her to her child. Even if she's away from her baby, working or running errands or out for an evening, a mother knows physically when it's time for a feeding and that her baby is hungry. They need each other. I loved that. So I had to know, would this baby want to nurse?

Yes, the doctor said, the baby would be hungry. And until the heart began to fail, he probably would be strong enough to nurse.

For some reason, that made me cry most of all.

~

Congenital heart defects are the leading cause of infant death from birth defects,[1] and hypoplastic left heart syndrome is the most severe congenital heart defect there is. Hypoplastic left heart syndrome is an umbrella term for a constellation of malformations on the left side of the heart, most notably a severely underdeveloped left ventricle, which is responsible after birth for pumping blood to every part of the body but the lungs. HLHS is also marked by an underdeveloped aorta, aortic valve, and mitral valve. (*Hypoplastic* refers to the arrested development of a part of the body.)

In plain English, these babies basically have half a heart. The left side simply will not be able to do its job.

Astonishingly for such a serious condition, babies with HLHS are healthy in the womb, because their mothers are supplying them with oxygen and because the left and right sides of the heart don't take on their distinct functions until after birth. While babies with HLHS are in the womb, the right side of the heart can compensate for problems on the left because the right side doesn't yet have to perform its job of supplying blood to the lungs. But after birth, the right side begins pumping blood only to the lungs, and the left side—which is supposed to be the stronger side—becomes responsible for pumping blood to the rest of the body and the brain. For most babies, this rerouting completes their transition to life outside the womb. In HLHS babies, unless they undergo surgical intervention first, it causes the blood supply to the body to be cut off. Instead of a transition to life, these babies make a transition to death.

HLHS occurs in one of about every five thousand births, affecting about a thousand babies in the United States every year.[2] About two-thirds of the affected babies are boys.[3] Researchers have been so far unable to pinpoint a cause of the defect, either genetic or environmental.

The term *hypoplastic left heart syndrome* was coined in 1958.[4] No treatment for the syndrome was available until around 1980, when Dr. William Norwood pioneered the surgery that now bears his name.[5] The

Norwood is performed within days of birth. In this surgery, the heart is rearranged so the right ventricle acts as the main pumping chamber, providing a mixture of oxygenated and unoxygenated blood to the body. Babies at this stage tend to look a little dusky or blue.[6] An intermediate surgery, which doctors added to the routine in 1989[7] and which has improved overall survival rates, is done at about six to nine months. The goal of this surgery is to reduce the workload of the right ventricle by diverting blood from the upper body so that it bypasses the heart and flows directly to the lungs.[8] The third stage, the Fontan, is generally performed around age two. After this surgery, nearly all the blood pumped out to the body passes through the lungs for oxygen first, resulting in toddlers who look pinker and healthier.[9]

Even if all three surgeries are successful, it's still a matter of seeing how long the right side of the heart holds out. The surgeries are only palliative, which means that they relieve the symptoms of the disease without curing it. They basically attempt to buy time until—if—doctors come up with a better treatment later.

Survival rates for HLHS infants who undergo the palliative surgeries have improved dramatically, although they vary significantly by hospital. On average, among the more than forty centers in the national Pediatric Cardiac Care Consortium, about half of the babies survive the first surgery.[10] High-volume centers have more survivors than hospitals that perform the complicated procedures less frequently. At the University of Michigan, for example, a leader in reconstructive surgery for HLHS, hospital survival after the first surgery has been reported at 76 percent.[11] And a recent study at the Children's Hospital of Philadelphia, where Dr. Norwood did his pioneering work, reported hospital survival after the first surgery at 71 percent. Of children who underwent the palliative surgeries at the Children's Hospital of Philadelphia between 1984 and 1988, only 28 percent were still alive by age three. But of those who underwent the surgeries there between 1995 and 1998, 66 percent made it to their third birthday.[12]

"The problem is, we just cannot get every child to the two or three best places in the country," one pediatric cardiologist told me. "It's the whole question of do the ends justify the means? Is the baby suffering?"

The operations require extraordinary skill on the part of surgeons, as they must rearrange hearts that are only about the size of a walnut. It is not uncommon for babies' hearts to be unable to start again after surgery, once they are off the heart-lung bypass machine, or for babies to go into cardiac arrest within days and never come home from the hospital.

In the mid-1990s, the staff at one Seattle hospital sent letters to the hospital's medical director and to the *Seattle Times* expressing alarm over watching so many babies die during Norwood attempts. An outside review of the hospital found no problems, noting that the death rate was consistent with the national average for the technically difficult procedure.[13]

One of the many HLHS experts I spoke with that hot summer acknowledged the numerous possible complications of the surgeries. I sat in our backyard, watching the girls splash in an inflatable wading pool and listening to the doctor on our portable phone. He mentioned that after the first surgery, some babies' hearts "just shut down." Feeding difficulties are "virtually universal" and frustrating for families, although "least medically concerning." The children are limited in how much they can exercise—T-ball would be OK, but high-endurance contact sports wouldn't be. Some children later need pacemakers or transplants. There is concern about long-term developmental and neurological problems, including learning disabilities and difficulties with speech and motor skills.

Given all that, however, he did not approve of comfort care.

"Knowing what I know now about long-term outcomes, I personally feel it's unethical not to intervene," he told me.

Others were more cautious. "More and more people are becoming less nihilistic," one heart surgeon told me. "By four to six, [the children] can be pretty normal." However, he added, "nobody knows what's going to happen long-term."

We also sought advice from pediatric cardiac nurses whose patients included babies with HLHS. Nurses are the ones who have the closest contact with these babies, around the clock after surgery and when they return to the hospital with complications. Granted, nurses have less contact with babies who do well and are sent home. But we found it telling that, having seen all they had seen, the nurses said they would opt for comfort care if it were their baby.

One nurse said that she had left three post-Norwood babies when her shift ended that day, and she knew that by the time she returned the next day, all three would be dead.

Another said, "There are some things worse than death."

We had three and a half months to sort through these conflicting medical opinions. It hardly seemed long enough. What must it be like for families who have only a few hours to decide?

A transplant seems like a promising option, like replacing a corroded car battery with a new one. Just hook up the cables and you're as good as new.

Especially for infants, it isn't nearly that easy. In the first place, finding a donor heart comes down to sheer luck. The heart needs to be small. About a thousand babies are born with HLHS every year in the United States,[14] while only about seventy infant donor hearts become available.[15] And those who die waiting for a heart must first endure significant intervention to try to keep them alive.

The world's first heart transplant in an infant was performed in 1967 in New York, just three days after Dr. Christiaan Barnard made history in South Africa by performing the first heart transplant in an adult. The baby lived six and a half hours. More than sixteen years passed before the second attempt, performed in 1984 in London on a baby girl with HLHS. She lived eighteen days after the surgery. In the third attempt, three months later, Dr. Leonard Bailey at Loma Linda University Medical Center in California transplanted a heart from a baboon into a baby girl who had HLHS and who became widely known as Baby Fae.[16] The operation made news around the world, inspiring awe as well as debate about the ethics of xenotransplantation and what was essentially an experiment on a human who was unable to give consent. Baby Fae lived for twenty days after the surgery.[17] Dr. Bailey performed the first successful infant-to-infant heart transplant, on a four-day-old boy with HLHS nicknamed Baby Moses, a year later.[18]

When children who receive heart transplants do survive, there is no guarantee of long-term success. Nationally, about two-thirds of all infant heart-transplant recipients are still alive five years later.[19] The body's natural defense of rejecting a foreign organ is a lifelong risk. And the antirejection drugs pose a Catch-22. Without them, the heart is rejected. With them, the immune system is suppressed so much that even a mild illness could be life threatening. Doctors do know that one possible side effect of the antirejection drugs is lymphoma—cancer— and that the arteries in donated hearts tend to harden early, necessitating another transplant later. (Transplanted hearts generally last about ten years.)[20] And an organ transplant in an infant is different from one in an adult; the antirejection drugs have significant stunting effects on a baby, whose physical and mental growth has barely begun.

"I don't think anybody knows whether we're doing these kids a favor long-term," one heart surgeon told me. He called heart transplants in infants "bad news."

On a practical level, transplants are done in only a few select medical centers, so parents often need to travel to a distant city to deliver their baby and wait for a heart, far from the support of family and friends.

One kind father spent a long time on the telephone with me, telling me about his four-year-old daughter's successful transplant. I could hear her playing happily in the background. It made my head spin. *Maybe our baby could be four!* A transplant is the way to go, he recommended. They had little time to decide, because their daughter's HLHS wasn't diagnosed until after birth. But they were able to visit with a couple whose son had undergone palliative surgery, and that was enough to turn them against it. He said that just crawling across the room left the little boy blue and short of breath.

But the details he related about the transplant, shared in the hope that we would choose a transplant over comfort care, had the opposite effect. Their daughter spent weeks in another city, along with four other babies, waiting for a heart and enduring extraordinary procedures to try to buy time. All the rest died without getting a heart. Instead of focusing on how lucky their daughter was, I felt so sorry for those other babies and their families. All that painful intervention, only to die far from home. I kept thinking, *I can't do that to our baby.* He confided that the antirejection drugs had stunted his daughter's growth and that they were hard on her kidneys. And finally, he said he needed to mention that when she was a toddler, the drugs caused her to get cancer. She underwent major surgery to remove the tumors, and the drugs were scaled back in an effort to avoid a recurrence of the cancer—leaving her at greater risk of rejection. And it's possible that her arteries will harden quickly, requiring her to need a new heart in ten years or so.

He was clearly a devoted, loving father, and that laughing little girl I heard over the phone was obviously the light of his life. All their medical difficulties paled in comparison to the joy of having her around.

But I can't do that to our baby.

❧

We are not medical Luddites. Living in this twenty-first century, hardly anyone can fail to be awed by the medicines and procedures available for countless diseases and injuries, treatments that were unimaginable just a few years ago. Generations of brilliant doctors and researchers and courageous patients have contributed to today's body of medical knowledge, which will soon be eclipsed by even more extraordinary discoveries.

But just because a medical course of action exists, is that reason enough to take it?

Our culture clings to a number of comforting myths about modern medicine, including the ideas that technology can fix everything and that finding a cure is just a matter of hauling oneself to the right hospital. Why don't you just go to the Mayo Clinic? Isn't there some experimental treatment in Mexico? If death does come, two corollary myths are that the patient didn't "fight" enough or that it was the doctors' fault.

We praise those who take every step possible, putting them on TV and in the newspapers, sustaining the myths and sometimes forgoing the follow-up stories. I read one newspaper story about a baby with HLHS who received a "miracle" transplant. The story said that the baby was doing well and had an 80 percent chance of survival.[21] I learned elsewhere that the baby died just a few weeks later.

As Deborah L. Davis, Ph.D., writes in *Loving and Letting Go:*

> Parents who turn away from aggressive medical intervention for their infants are sometimes scorned in this age of high technology and incredible advances. There is a lot of social pressure to "go for it" and use the best technology that medicine offers. . . . [P]arents who choose non-intervention can feel put on the defensive, even though by some standards, theirs was the more heroic decision. Indeed, it is much harder to let go than to hold on. These are the parents who

have the courage to let go and meet death, with tears and clenched fists, but on some level accepting what is inevitable for all of us.[22]

We feared setting our baby off on a spiral of medical complications, one problem daisy-chained to the next, keeping him tethered to the medical system for the rest of his life. Maybe we too needed to heed the ancient admonition still given to doctors today: *Primum non nocere.* First, do no harm.

It would be one thing to welcome into our family a baby who was born needing special care but who was otherwise able to stay alive. But what if futile attempts to keep our baby alive only caused him to die in an agony he couldn't possibly understand? What if we thwarted death only to end up causing our child to have difficulty eating, breathing, or even thinking? Would fending off death at every step of the way be for his benefit or for ours, all because we couldn't bear to accept the reality of his unfixable heart?

❦

I spent many late-night hours searching the Internet, which of course is littered with hearsay but also offers a wealth of information. It is a bountiful new resource for information on rare medical conditions such as

HLHS. I could find nothing on the topic in our city library system, while quick Internet searches found thousands of entries. Some were refereed medical sites, while others were sites developed by organizations devoted to congenital heart defects.

Many families also posted their personal stories on the Internet. They were no more statistically significant or medically accurate than conversations overheard at a restaurant. But they were exceptionally compelling to me, as they were filled with journal entries, details about hospital stays, and minutiae about what the babies were eating and even how much they were throwing up. (And it was a lot. Their tiny rearranged hearts could not provide enough oxygen for normal digestion.) I read them for hours. Many families posted wrenching photographs of beautiful, unconscious babies attached to tubes and machines. One even posted a picture of a sedated baby lying on his back with his chest wound open, the incision still too swollen from the surgery to be sutured shut. Some Web sites offered pictures of toddlers who, to my eyes, looked pale and blue. Some babies' Web sites were decorated with images of Tigger and Pooh; far too many others featured pictures of angels, for children who had died.

Although I felt a little voyeuristic reading these stories from the anonymity of my home computer, I am grateful to all those who put their stories online. We learned dozens of babies' stories this way, without getting pressure from parents to decide one way or another and without intruding on strangers' grief.

A few stories gave us fleeting hope. The children were well enough to splash in the tub, play on the computer, and go to Disneyland (using a special disability pass because they tired easily).

But some sites replaced our hope with resignation. There were postings from parents distraught over problems with feeding tubes or by their heart baby's exhaustion from simply trying to suck on a bottle. Many babies were too small to register on their pediatrician's growth chart. Some celebratory postings announced that parents had been able to get their toddler to eat a spoonful of tomato soup or to swallow a Cheerio without gagging or spitting it out. (Children who are tube-fed—for months or sometimes years—must learn later how to eat and what it means to feel hunger.) Food is one of life's greatest needs and pleasures; babies should not have to struggle to eat.

Some sites would boast about miracle children and how great the "little fighters" were doing while downplaying extra surgeries, diaphragms or vocal cords paralyzed by surgery, chest pain that was frightening to the child, or learning disabilities perhaps caused by long-term low oxygen levels.

Even grimmer were the stories of babies who survived one or more of the surgeries only to suffer a debilitating stroke on the operating room table during a subsequent surgery—still tallied as a success in hospital statistics—or who died during a routine presurgery heart catheterization.

We wondered if HLHS children would ever be out of the woods. Could their parents ever trust that their child's heart would continue to beat? More important, if the children grew old enough to understand their condition, could they ever truly trust their own heart either?

◈

Someone finally phoned with the results from the amniocentesis. Mark and I picked up separate extensions so that we could listen together. Good news, she said. Everything looked perfectly normal.

I stared at the black and white square tiles of our kitchen floor, feeling hollow. Everything else about our baby was perfect. This was supposed to be good news? Why not the one thing he really needed? Why not his heart?

We asked if the test also had confirmed the baby's gender. We had wanted to hear this news in a birthing room filled with joy and laughter and the cries of a healthy baby.

"It's a boy," we heard over the phone.

We had a son.

❧

We decided to name him Gabriel.

Naming a baby who has died or may die is even more complicated than naming a healthy baby. Parents often wonder if they should save a favorite name for a possible future child and find another name for their dying child. But many decide that the name they had in mind rightfully belongs to this baby, no matter how long the baby will live. That was our feeling too.

The name Gabriel has obvious heavenly connotations, and most people assume that's why we chose it. Its association with angels made it all the more fitting. But that wasn't our initial reason for choosing the name. Gabriel had been our leading contender for boys' names ever since I was pregnant with Elena. That summer, Mark and I traveled to Europe, where Mark enjoyed his comparative beer studies and we scoured everything for ideas for baby names. Museums, menus, street signs, and overheard conversations were all fair game. We were especially interested in Eastern European names because Mark's last name, Neuzil, is Czech.

One bright afternoon, we were strolling across the famous fourteenth-century Charles Bridge over the Vltava River in Prague. It was several years after the fall of the Communist regime, and entrepreneurial artists had set up shop along the bridge connecting Lesser Town and Old Town, selling jewelry and etchings and watercolors.

The waist-high stone walls of the bridge are topped with towering, soot-darkened baroque statues of saints. We stopped to admire one of them, a statue engraved with the name of the archangel Gabriel.

Gabriel. Gabriel Neuzil. That was it! We had found a boy name. It seemed strong and lyrical, and Mark could imagine it being announced at a basketball game just as easily as I could picture it listed on a concert program.

Never in our darkest nightmares would we have imagined it chiseled into a gravestone.

❦

Abortion was not suggested to us directly, although we still could have obtained one legally. Minnesota law allows abortions during the first half of pregnancy for any reason and during the second half to preserve the life or health of the mother,[23] which can be interpreted very broadly. One local abortion clinic performs elective abortions through approximately twenty-two weeks of pregnancy. At the time of the diagnosis, Gabriel was already three weeks older than that. However, we knew we could travel to another state for a legal "partial-birth" abortion (which even the American Medical Association has called "a procedure we all agree is not good medicine").[24]

But Gabriel's life was probably going to be far too short as it was. Why would we cut his life even shorter? And if we were considering protecting him from painful surgeries intended to help him, surely we would protect him from a painful, aggressive act intended to kill him. It was beyond horrific to think that Gabriel's only contact with humans outside the womb could be with the gloved hands of a stranger paid to kill him by grabbing his little feet and ramming scissors into the base of his skull.

∾

We had spoken with doctors, nurses, and families. We also needed to talk with an expert of another realm.

We do not consider ourselves devout; spiritually intrigued and institutionally skeptical would be a better description. (We joke that some reporters can't seem to type the word *Catholic* without preceding it with *devout,* as though the phrase is stored under the F1 key on their computer.) But we hoped the teachings and traditions of our church might also offer us some guidance.

I called the rectory of our new parish, where we hadn't met any of the priests yet, and left a voice-mail message for one of them. I said I was six months pregnant with a baby who had a fatal heart condition and asked if we could please come talk with him sometime.

A few days later we found ourselves sitting in Father Bill Baer's office, which was adorned with a replica of the San Damiano cross and also needed a good coat of paint. He had an easy smile and a quick wit as we chatted a bit about his former career as an architect. It probably would have been an enjoyable visit in other circumstances. Then he settled in behind his desk with his omnipresent glass of Coca-Cola and invited us to share our story.

We started in on our abridged explanation of HLHS. After only two weeks, we had it down pretty well.

"Have you heard of it?" I asked Father Baer during a pause in Mark's recitation, mostly to be polite. Hardly anybody has heard of HLHS, aside from people in the medical field.

"I was wondering if that's what your baby has," he replied.

Of all people, we had stumbled across—or been led to?—a priest who knew a great deal about HLHS. He had studied it, he knew about Dr. Norwood and the palliative surgeries, and he had even consulted with theologians about the medical ethics involved in treating the condition or deciding not to treat.

My emotions were spinning like a centrifuge.

He's going to tell us we should operate.

He prayed with us, saying Gabriel's name reverently. He listened to our story while Mark and I depleted his supply of Kleenex. Soon he was dialing a number on the phone, calling a mother of a child living with HLHS.

"I think you should give your baby a chance," she told me over the phone.

Our visit nearing its end, he told us he would be there for us whenever we needed him and would try to answer any questions we might have.

Finally getting to the heart of the matter, I said we did have one urgent question. I told him that the main reason we came to talk with him was that we wanted to know if the church would consider surgical intervention in Gabriel's case to be "extraordinary means." While the Catholic Church strives to be a strong voice in defense of life—for the unborn, the infirm, the condemned, the poor—the church also teaches that one is not obligated to undertake extraordinary medical means in order to sustain life. The church also draws a sharp ethical line between withholding extraordinary treatment, thus allowing death to come naturally, and taking direct actions intended to end a life. You might say that the church does not insist on artificially maintaining life at all costs, but it does insist on *reverence* for life at all costs.

Slicing open the chest, sawing through the breastbone. Three times. All for no cure.

"It just seems like too much to ask of a baby," I said tearfully.

He seemed to draw himself up a bit taller in his chair.

"I can tell you, as Christ's representative to you on this earth," he began, "that you have no moral obligation to operate."

❦

No one can fashion a whole heart out of half of one.

As we waded through all the statistics about survival rates, percentages of this and risks of that, we began to focus on other statistics that were unspoken. It became increasingly clear to us that even with surgeries—assuming Gabriel lived through them in the first place—his chances of getting a normally functioning, reliable heart were zero. His chances of unimaginable pain and a lifetime of uncertainty: 100 percent.

Call it pessimism or lack of faith in doctors or lack of faith in God, but we also did not believe that Gabriel would survive the surgeries. It seemed to us that the Solomonic choice we were being asked to make on behalf of our son was not between life and death but between a painful death and a peaceful one.

With broken hearts of our own, we decided to forgo medical intervention for our beautiful baby and his imperfect heart.

In our view, comfort care did not mean that we would do nothing. We felt we would be parenting him in another profound way: we would be protecting him from the medical onslaught.

Our doctors and nurses, especially the nurses, understood. One told us that she thought we would find peace in knowing that we were sparing our baby from being turned into a "science experiment."

Said another, very kindly and with tears in her eyes, "You're going to love him to death."

No one could give Gabriel a good heart. So we set out to give him a good life.

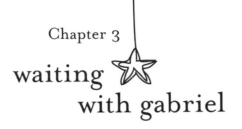

Chapter 3

waiting with gabriel

HOW WAS I SUPPOSED TO walk around pregnant for three and a half more months, knowing our baby was going to die? How could I even go to the grocery store and have a cashier ask casually when my baby was due?

I have to admit that in the first dark day or two after Gabriel's diagnosis, I thought it would be something of a relief if the amniocentesis caused me to go into premature labor right away, a possible complication of the test.

But even though I was the one walking around pregnant, I also was favored with constant reminders that Gabriel was still alive and safe inside of me. Every time

I lay down to sleep, his squirms and kicks said hello. I could tell when he had the hiccups. I could nudge my stomach to try to make him move, and I could try to guess which part of him I was touching. Was that his head, or his undoubtedly adorable little butt? As he grew and settled into position for birth, I could almost always feel one of his little feet just to the right of my navel. No matter where I went, I could take him with me. And when the grief came crashing over me, I could seek solace in curling around him. Among all the people being affected by Gabriel's expected death, I began to feel like the fortunate one.

I thought many times of our friends Tom and Jean, whose daughter Claire was born and died almost exactly two years before Gabriel's due date. Claire had a fatal chromosomal problem, which her parents also learned about before her birth. They handled the remainder of their pregnancy with such grace. Claire lived for one hour and died in her father's arms. I remembered something Jean had said: that she cherished each day she was still pregnant, because she knew her daughter was still alive.

I also returned again and again to Web pages by two mothers of babies with HLHS who continued their pregnancies and also chose compassionate care.

"Don't be afraid, for you are not alone," began the page in memory of Alex, a beautiful little boy with a full head of black hair. "Over the painful months of my pregnancy, we prayed for a miracle, sadly believing that none had been bestowed upon us. Gratefully, we came to realize that God had given us a miracle: Alex would be born."

And this, from the mother of a wise-looking newborn named Daniel who lived for five days: "The five months of 'knowing' were not easy, yet I am forever thankful that I knew. The time I had allowed me to prepare so that we could enjoy each and every second we had with Daniel. . . . We were filled with such joy and love. In a very bittersweet way, those days with Daniel were certainly the best in our lives; we were a complete family."

Both pages were posted at a Web site for parents who continued their pregnancies after receiving a devastating fatal diagnosis. The site was titled "Waiting with Love."

Waiting with love.

It gave us words for exactly what we wanted to do.

 ❧

If it seemed cruel for parents to face losing a child, it seemed infinitely crueler for little children to lose their baby brother.

41

On that first morning after the diagnosis, Elena sat quietly at the kitchen table while I gave her breakfast and tried to talk about normal things.

She picked at her breakfast and said sadly, "I thought we were going to be able to keep the new baby for a long time."

"I thought so too," I said.

"But I wanted a new baby," she said.

᭜

We went through the litany with the girls countless times. They would peer into our eyes, looking for tears, and ask, "Mommy, why are you sad?" (Or, later, just "Daddy, are you sad?") Because Gabriel has a sick heart. Why does he have a sick heart? We don't know. It just grew that way.

We explained again and again that because of Gabriel's sick heart, after he was born his body would stop working and his spirit would go to be with God. And we always made sure to repeat that Mommy had a perfect heart, Daddy had a perfect heart, Elena had a perfect heart, Maria had a perfect heart . . . adding anybody else they happened to see that day.

I remember taking the girls shopping one day for new swimming suits. I had picked out one for each of them, but Maria kept insisting on picking out a third for the "new baby." Exasperated, Elena finally said, "Maria, the new baby's not going to live that long." Oh, right.

Their childlike acceptance helped us accept it as well. Mommy and Daddy said Gabriel was not going to live, so that was that. And the girls had a basic understanding of death, with my grandmother Cecilia Kuebelbeck having died at age ninety-four just a week before Gabriel's diagnosis. We brought the girls to her funeral and let them gently touch her hands at the wake, explaining that she didn't need her body anymore and her spirit was with God. She had loved children; in her final years just about the only thing that could briefly part the fog of Alzheimer's was the sight of a baby. I think she would have been pleased to have small children at her funeral.

Well-meaning people at a loss for something to say would sometimes tell us to be grateful for the children we already had. I never knew how to respond to that. It seemed like such a non sequitur, like telling someone whose house just burned down, "Be grateful you still have your legs." Of course the imminent loss of Gabriel made us even more grateful for our girls. But he was a separate child. And watching his sisters play and grow and laugh reminded us all too sharply of what we would be missing without him.

Having said that, to be honest, our other children were our lifelines. We still had little ones to care for, to read bedtime stories to, to kiss when they fell, to tickle and chase and cuddle and rock to sleep. I can barely begin to imagine the heartache of parents who lose their only child.

❧

Within hours of the diagnosis, help began pouring in. Food. Flowers. Cards. Phone calls, so many phone calls. All those wonderful people who mustered the courage to call, even if all they could say was that they didn't know what to say.

My parents came to be with us that first weekend, bearing homemade soup and bags stuffed with groceries. Mark and my dad went to the lumberyard and then performed therapeutic hammering and sawing, building a swing set in our backyard in a single day. By suppertime, the girls were shrieking with delight on their new swings. My sister Jane spent her birthday with me. My mom and my sister Molly showed up on my doorstep one of those first Saturdays, bearing buckets and cleaning supplies and freshly cut yellow tulips from Molly's yard. One of Mark's aunts, an enthusiastic gardener, took a lengthy Greyhound bus ride to help us plant snapdragons and impatiens and tend to our roses and daylilies. Mark's parents drove from Iowa to be with us. Mark's sister Beth and her husband, Bob, flew in from St. Louis to see us, and Bob did his best to make our lawn look as manicured as his. From Cincinnati came Mark's brother Paul and his pregnant wife, Amy. Coworkers sent cards, worked overtime until I could return to my editing responsibilities at the Associated Press, and stepped in to teach some of Mark's classes at the University of St. Thomas. People we didn't even know were praying for us, as our names were put on prayer lists at various churches of various faiths.

This child who had not yet taken a breath was already inspiring an outpouring of caring and support and love.

❧

By the door of the high-risk maternity center at our hospital was a discreet display of pamphlets for parents whose hope for a particular pregnancy has been extinguished. I took one from the Pregnancy and Infant Loss Center, a trailblazing group in Minnesota that has since been folded into other organizations. I remembered reading about the group before, back when infant loss happened to other people, not to me.

I hoped that the group might help me find other parents who had learned of their baby's HLHS before birth and had decided to provide comfort care. An understanding woman answered the phone when I called, asked about our baby, and listened without interrupting while I explained Gabriel's heart condition and occasionally set the phone down to get more Kleenex. Only then did she share that she knew all about HLHS because her own son had died of it thirteen years previously. We talked for a long time, and she said she would pass my name along to a local volunteer who also had faced HLHS in her family.

A woman named Robin called me the next day. She said she had been wondering what she should do to honor what would have been her son's third birthday when she came home and found a message from the Pregnancy and Infant Loss Center on her answering machine. So instead of throwing a party for John, her little boy, she spent part of his birthday calling me, listening, and sharing their story.

They had experienced double heartbreak: two children with HLHS. Their daughter, Corinne, was not diagnosed until after birth. She lived for fifteen hours. When they wanted to try again, their perinatologist—who was also ours—told them not to worry, because she had never seen this kind of lightning strike twice. Their son John was diagnosed before birth and lived for three days, dying peacefully at home.

Robin said that because they didn't know about their daughter's heart ahead of time, they were able to have a happy pregnancy. But they have few clear memories of her after she was born because of the medical whirlwind and the shock. As difficult as it was to know ahead of time about their son, she said they preferred it, because they were able to plan ahead, research the treatments, and shower all their love on him once he arrived.

Robin called me several times throughout the rest of my pregnancy, more frequently as the due date drew nearer. Talking with someone who had lived through the same situation was such a gift.

I also devoured newsletters and other reading materials about infant death, reading and crying in our living room after everyone else was in bed. Particularly heartbreaking was a photograph in the booklet *When Hello Means Goodbye* of a couple tenderly dressing their stillborn son. Visible in the photograph was the baby's tiny hand, perfect and limp.

Oh, Gabriel. I hadn't yet thought about seeing your little hands.

Other parents' heartrending stories helped foreshadow what might happen with us and gave us ideas for honoring Gabriel's short life. At least when it came time to caress Gabriel's hands, or give him his final bath, or close the casket, I would have done it in my mind first. The stories helped light our path. And they showed us it was possible to make it through to the other side.

☙

After the diagnosis, I remembered reading in one of the metro newspapers about a local company that sold literature and other materials for people facing a crisis in pregnancy or infant death.[1] One of the owners started the company as a branch of his publishing business after his daughter was stillborn and he realized that few resources existed for people suffering similar losses. I even ordered a catalog once after a friend had a miscarriage. At the time, I paged through it, scanning the book titles and gazing at the birth-death announcement cards, thinking that it was the saddest thing I had ever seen.

Now I needed it for myself. I dug through my papers, and sure enough I had saved it all those months. Reading it was even more heartbreaking this time. There was a slender baby book specifically for babies who die, because no bereaved parent wants a regular off-the-shelf baby book with pages to record firsts that will forever remain empty. This book featured the usual pages on which to record the baby's family tree and birth statistics, along with pages for handprints, footprints, and a lock of hair. But it also had a page on which to paste a funeral program and a page with a heartbreaking fill-in-the-blank sentence that read, "Our baby died on _____."

I was especially drawn to the birth-death announcement cards. Now there's something you won't find at the shopping mall. The cards seemed to me to be a sensitive and tangible way to let people know about Gabriel, in the unimaginable future after he had arrived and then left us. The illustrations were understated and touching. One featured a red-gold maple tree with a lone leaf drifting away. On another, a man's hand had just released a sunset orange balloon into a blue summer sky.

I turned the page and saw a striking watercolor of a child's hand touching the palm of an ethereal hand of God. It reminded me of Michelangelo's *Creation of Adam* from the Sistine Chapel ceiling, especially now that the frescoes have been restored to their original vibrant hues. The inscription on the card read: "Let the children come to me! Do not stop them, because the Kingdom of God belongs to such as these."

I knew at that moment that I wanted to use that illustration and that Gospel passage to announce Gabriel's birth. It suited our circumstances perfectly. We were going to let Gabriel come to God.

❧

There is no good era in which to lose a child, although times in the past have been much worse.

A friend once told me that her grandmother felt so forbidden to grieve over the death of her baby that sometimes, when the grandmother couldn't stand it anymore, she would slip out of her farmhouse, flee far enough into the cornfield to where she thought no one could hear, and scream.

Tragically, infant death often was—and in too many places still is—greatly minimized. Especially once childbirth became the province of hospitals, by the 1940s and 1950s, stillborn babies and babies who died shortly after birth often were whisked away while their mothers were still sedated and exhausted from childbirth.[2] Parents were not allowed to see or hold their dead babies, partly out of hospital workers' misguided belief that it would be too distressing. An obstetric nursing textbook from the 1950s said nothing about how to care for parents experiencing stillbirth or neonatal death, but it did refer to babies with birth defects as "monsters." "Parents should not be allowed to see monstrosities," the authors wrote.[3] Even into the 1980s, many hospitals still prohibited parents from seeing or holding their stillborn babies.[4] Mothers and fathers were deprived of their only chance to parent their child. Mothers were told to simply forget about that baby and have another one, as if children were interchangeable. Parents were made to feel that naming the baby was morbid and unnecessary. Discussing infant death became taboo.

The babies' bodies often were buried hurriedly, with only the father or a few witnesses present, while the mother was still in the hospital recuperating. Sometimes the bodies were buried by the hospital in unmarked common graves. Some hospitals sent babies' bodies to funeral homes to be buried anonymously in a casket together with an unrelated adult.[5] Even today, bodies sometimes are unceremoniously incinerated and dumped in landfills along with the hospital's medical waste.

Too often, the babies were never spoken of again. As Elisabeth Kübler-Ross once said,

> Our present Western society is not willing to experience death, in the sense that it is hidden by a conspiracy of silence. The sudden and unexplained death of a baby is very tragic, yet it is not regarded as something to be sad over, especially if the baby has never lived. As a consequence, parents are often not given permission by family or friends to mourn the death of their baby, and they are very often left alone in an apparently unsympathetic world, not knowing how to feel and not knowing how to cope.[6]

For infants as well as adults, the end of life and the journey of grief have been taken out of the home and now exist in the realm of hospitals and funeral homes. Most people today say they would prefer to die at home if possible, but most don't. Wakes in the home used to be common but are virtually unheard of these days. Most people today have never witnessed a death, and many have never even seen a dead body. For many of us, our relationship with death is mediated by macabre images from Hollywood and Halloween.

Back when death was better integrated into the rhythms and realities of everyday life, babies who died were sometimes honored, mourned, and remembered. Wandering around old cemeteries, you can still find elaborate angel monuments to babies who died. Many of the babies were named. And photographing babies after death was once a common part of mourning.[7]

My late Grandma Kuebelbeck had a baby sister, Teresa, the tenth of fifteen children, who died shortly after being born at the family's farmhouse in the summer of 1925. She died of an umbilical-cord problem, despite the efforts of a doctor who made a house call for the birth. Decades afterward, Grandma displayed in her home small locket-sized photographs of all her siblings, including a photograph of her baby sister in her tiny casket. Another sister, Marie, recalled—nearly eighty years later—details of the baby's wake: the baby was dressed in a delicate white dress, she was laid out in the casket in the family's parlor on a small table by a window, and relatives and neighbors came by to offer their sympathies. Marie, who was twelve at the time, remembered being sent by their mother to the home of some nearby bachelor farmers to ask for flowers for the baby. She returned home with armloads of petunias, lavender and pink and white. "When they heard a baby died, they did everything they could to help us," she said.

The entire family, children included, went to the cemetery for the graveside blessing. "She was a cute little baby," Marie recalled. "We all remembered her always through the years. I have never forgotten any of that."

The relatively recent minimization of infant death coincided with the medicalization of birth, as doctors (generally male) superseded lay midwives (generally female). This eventually led to dramatically lower rates of maternal and newborn deaths and to other welcome advances, such as pain relief and cesarean sections. Personally, I wouldn't consider giving birth today outside of a hospital; I want all that expertise and equipment down the hall just in case. But the medicalization of birth also had its excesses and disasters, including the highly efficient transmission of the fatal puerperal, or childbed, fever, which was spread by practitioners who failed to wash their hands between patients or even after performing autopsies. (At the Vienna Lying-In Hospital in the 1840s, maternal mortality rates fell significantly after Dr. Ignaz Semmelweiss insisted that his skeptical staff wash their hands in chloride of lime after dissecting bodies and before examining laboring women.)[8] As time passed, husbands were banished from delivery rooms, forced to leave their often unprepared and frightened wives alone with masked doctors and nurses, who performed their tasks under blinding lights in sterile hospital rooms. Women were literally strapped to the delivery table, their arms in cuffs and their feet in stirrups. All the while, hospital births became the norm. In 1900, less than 5 percent of all American babies were born in hospitals. By 1939, it was up to 50 percent, and by 1970, it was at nearly 100 percent.[9]

Parents eventually rebelled. They demanded that fathers be allowed to share in that most intimate, wondrous moment when their children would emerge from the womb and give out their first cry. They pressed for natural childbirth, childbirth education classes, more homelike birth settings within hospitals, and an assortment of other innovations, such as whirlpool baths to soothe labor pains and even birthing tubs for giving birth underwater. They sought to have hospital births attended by nurse-midwives, who generally have a less interventionist approach and are able to spend much more time with a laboring woman (but who also are usually affiliated with physicians who can help with nonroutine developments).

Like those who sought to reclaim respect for childbirth as a natural process rather than as a medical procedure, some people are now attempting to do the same with death. A nascent "dying well" movement is emphasizing dignity, hospice care, better pain management, and other approaches that allow for the profound spiritual and emotional growth that can happen at the end of life—both for the person who is dying and for the ones left behind.

Similarly, we are now also on the cusp of a significant cultural shift regarding infant death. Parents are beginning to be encouraged to cherish and honor their children in tangible ways, and they are finally being allowed to grieve. Driven by the persistent efforts of bereaved parents, who began actively seeking reform in the 1970s, many hospitals have adopted more sensitive practices and offer support groups and professional counselors for parents who experience miscarriage and infant death. Efforts also are under way to improve care for parents who experience losses earlier in pregnancy; for example, some parents are lobbying for hospitals to provide options other than routine incineration for disposing of babies' remains. Several national organizations now exist, including the National SHARE

Pregnancy and Infant Loss Support, founded in 1977 by Sister Jane Marie Lamb, O.S.F., and now based in St. Charles, Missouri. The Compassionate Friends group exists for parents who have lost a child of any age.

Inspired by Richard Paul Evans's best-selling book *The Christmas Box,* about a fictional woman mourning at the angel monument that marks her young daughter's grave, communities around the globe are erecting angel statues as memorials to babies who have died. Memorial sites like these are giving parents—especially those who do not have a gravesite to visit—a physical place to grieve. Even parents whose babies died many years ago are seeking out these memorials for solace, grateful that after so much time someone is finally acknowledging their loss and their sorrow.

Fewer parents today must endure the death of a baby. The infant mortality rate has dropped considerably in the United States since the early 1900s, when an estimated 10 percent of all babies died before their first birthday. The rate is now less than 1 percent. But that still represents a lot of babies—and a lot of grieving parents. About twenty-eight thousand infants a year die before their first birthday.[10] About a million U.S. pregnancies end in miscarriage or stillbirth every year,[11] with about twenty-seven thousand of those babies dying during the second half of pregnancy.[12]

In part because of the loving work of parents whose profound loss was minimized or ignored in the past, many newly bereaved parents are now encouraged to hold their child's body and to view that tender act as healthy and natural. They are invited to create memories with their child: to rock their baby, to give their baby a name, and to take photographs of their baby. If the idea of taking photographs is too painful for the parents to contemplate, hospital staff sometimes take pictures and keep them on file in case parents want to see them later. Nurses help parents collect priceless mementos such as handprints, footprints, and a lock of hair. Parents are encouraged to hold a memorial service of some kind and to wait until the mother is physically able to attend.

Caregivers are often awed by parents' capacity to love the pure essence of their child, even if the baby has obvious physical malformations. Many parents are able to acknowledge their baby's physical imperfections while also lovingly noticing the parts that formed perfectly, perhaps long eyelashes, graceful fingers, a nose like Mom's or a chin like Dad's.

These parents will not be leaving the hospital with a baby, but unlike far too many heartbroken mothers and fathers in the past, they will at least be recognized as parents of a unique, irreplaceable child.

We were not abandoned.

We were very lucky.

Because death has been relegated to hospitals and funeral homes, many people are so uncomfortable with and unaccustomed to death that they don't know what to do when death comes calling. Far-flung families can't always attend funerals, and we've lost some of the rituals and etiquette that guided us during those awkward, painful times. For fear of saying the wrong thing, people sometimes say nothing or stay away completely, leaving survivors even more isolated in their grief. As anthropologist Margaret Mead once wrote:

> Mourning has become unfashionable in the United States. The bereaved are supposed to pull themselves together as quickly as possible and to reweave the torn fabric of life. . . . We do not allow . . . for the weeks and months during which a loss is realized—a beautiful word that suggests the transmutation of the strange into something that is one's own. [13]

When the person who has died is a baby, it adds another layer of shock. It violates the natural order as well as contemporary assumptions that as long as the mother does all the "right" things—avoids alcohol, takes prenatal vitamins, follows the Best-Odds Diet—the product in nine months will be a healthy baby.

We lived in a strange twilight of grief while we waited for Gabriel to be born, as many families do during the last stages of a family member's fatal illness. Many wonderful people were willing to wait in that twilight with us. Our phone rang often, with my mom and five sisters checking in and probably bracing themselves for what would surely be a long, tearful monologue from me. Our friends Barb and Gene invited us over often so all our kids could play and we could talk. We'd visit my parents and swim in their pool and find ourselves crying again. A group of mothers from an early-childhood class made sure to include me and the girls in play dates at parks and in backyards all summer. My sister Karen organized prayers on our behalf. Our friends Tom and Jean made it a point to call on Mother's Day, remembering how difficult that day was for them while they were awaiting their daughter's birth and death.

Help came from unexpected places too. One afternoon I took the girls to the neighborhood library to see if it had anything on HLHS or infant death. The girls were darting through the children's book section, bringing various books to me and asking me to read them, while I stood at a computer and typed keywords into the database. Searches of the entire city library system's holdings were turning up nothing.

One of the librarians, a woman who led story times and puppet shows for young children, came up and asked if I needed help finding anything. I almost said no thanks, satisfied that I had done a fairly comprehensive search. But after hesitating a moment, I told her what I was looking for and why.

She flew into action, consulting medical indexes and other references. She didn't find much either, but there was one book she thought might be of interest to me. Rather than simply writing the Dewey decimal number on a slip of paper and handing it to me, she escorted me and the girls back into the stacks to help me find it.

At the far end of the row, flanked by books, she turned to me with tears in her eyes.

"I lost a baby too," she said.

Twelve years earlier, her daughter was born with osteogenesis imperfecta, or brittle-bone disease. The little girl never came home from the hospital and lived for only a few days.

The librarian wanted to do something to help. Could she make us a meal or something? I was so taken aback by this kindness from a complete stranger that I politely declined. She really wanted to do something, though, so she thought for a moment and remembered a short book that had been helpful to her. The library did not carry it, and she decided that it should. So she said she was going to order the book for the library, pay for it herself, and put my name first on the call list.

Someone from the library called a few weeks later to say that my requested book was in. It took me another couple of weeks to work up the energy to go pick it up. I walked to the checkout counter along with my girls and asked the librarian on duty if it was still on hold. She couldn't find it. Within moments the librarian from my earlier visit was there too, having seen us walk through the door. She had tucked the book away for me and knew just where it was.

I got out my library card and noticed that the book had no library identification label on it.

No, take it, she said. I bought another one for the library. This one is for you.

She was no longer a complete stranger. She was another mother grieving for her baby, just like me.

༁

During one of our meetings with Father Baer, he said that people experiencing great sorrow some- times tell him that, strangely, it gives them glimpses of heaven. He seemed to suggest this carefully, as though he was bracing himself for a potentially explosive response. *Heaven?! What kind of ivory tower do you live in? My baby is going to die. This isn't heaven; this is pure hell.* If someone had insensitively suggested this to us too soon after the diagnosis, that might have been our reaction. But we understood what he meant. We were already overwhelmed and humbled by the cumulative effect of people's gestures of love and support. Strand by strand, we were being enveloped—to borrow novelist Jon Hassler's phrase—in "a cocoon of goodness."

∾

To tell or not to tell? That was the awkward question we had to ask ourselves when strangers and distant acquaintances were involved.

An obvious pregnancy is as natural a topic for small talk as the weather. "When's your baby due?" "Do you know if you're having a boy or a girl?" Of course we got those questions too. We decided generally that if the questioner were someone we would need to see again, we would relate a brief version of the story. Sometimes we assumed wrongly that people had already heard the news through the grapevine, leading to uncomfortable exchanges. Other times we tried to accept people's congratulations graciously. In a way it was nice to have people acknowledge our baby without their comments being tinged with sympathy.

One oppressively hot July evening, we went to a St. Paul Saints game. Or, as we thought of it, we took our son to a baseball game. The Saints, a minor-league team, play in a low-budget outdoor stadium to sellout crowds who love the team's pig mascot and general spirit of raucous self-deprecation.

I hope Gabriel appreciated it, because I was miserable. My ankles ballooned. I don't even *like* baseball. But it was good for Mark. We went with friends, and Mark got to cheer and laugh and talk about something else for a couple of hours. And for a while I got to act like any other sweltering pregnant woman.

"You having a boy or a girl?" shouted someone a couple of rows back, over the din of the crowd and the announcer and the guy hawking hot dogs.

"A boy!" I shouted back.

❧

We tried to give the girls, and ourselves, as normal a summer as possible. Many times we spoke of doing something "with Gabriel." We took him fishing on a secluded lake near the North Shore of Lake Superior, not far from Ely, where Mark was teaching a summer environmental studies course. I took Gabriel swinging on the girls' backyard swings. We took him to a Minnesota Twins game at the Metrodome (Mark's idea) and to a concert by the male vocal ensemble Chanticleer at Orchestra Hall (mine). I had returned to the Associated Press two weeks after the diagnosis, but my wonderfully understanding supervisors made it possible for me to step away eight weeks before the due date, giving us priceless time to spend our bittersweet summer as a complete family.

⁓

Prenatal appointments always sent us plummeting back into reality. All it would take was our kind nurse Sandra to ask how we were doing, and I'd be saying, "Fine" while simultaneously reaching for her Kleenex. Especially because I knew what normal prenatal visits would be like—listening to the baby's heartbeat, measuring my abdomen, talking cheerily about each stage of the baby's development—these visits were heartbreakingly empty. Nothing to do except check my blood pressure. No point in even checking the baby.

⁓

There were the inevitable platitudes about God "needing another angel" or God "taking" Gabriel from us for a reason. I can't imagine those concepts being a comfort to anybody. What kind of sadistic god would breathe life into a baby only to snuff it out? After millennia of infant deaths, you'd think God would have plenty. If God needed more babies in heaven, God could simply will some into existence. Or God could take a baby being poisoned before birth with alcohol and cocaine, or a baby who will be thrown into a dumpster or left for dead in a filthy public bathroom. I would be bitter for the rest of my life—and probably beyond—if I thought a higher power had targeted my baby to die. (And, to get picky, theological teachings say that humans who die do not turn into angels.)

Fortunately, we had already stumbled across the idea that God was grieving *with* us. God was not taking Gabriel, but God the Mother and Father of all would lovingly receive him. As the waves of grief tossed us end over end, slamming our faces into the sand, we clung to the belief that God was not abandoning Gabriel or us. We desperately needed to believe that this sparrow would not fall unnoticed.

It helped to think of Gabriel's heart as a tragic consequence of an imperfect world, one in which people sometimes staggeringly misuse their free will and in which little hearts sometimes form incomplete.

❧

Although it was rather late to be buying maternity clothes, I decided about six weeks before Gabriel's due date that I deserved a new sundress to help lift my spirits during the hot summer days that lay ahead.

The girls giggled and played quietly in the clothing racks while I browsed. We were the only people in the store other than an older employee who looked like a manager and a younger employee who offered to keep an eye on the girls while I went into the dressing room.

After rejecting stacks of dresses, I finally found one I liked—black, sleeveless, with small ivory flowers—and that I thought made my stomach look only moderately huge. Triumph!

As I wrote out my check, the older worker asked whether I was "done" having children, in a tone of voice that suggested that three was more than enough. I was caught off-guard by the personal nature of the question and by the implied criticism. You'd think a maternity store would welcome customers who continued to have children. Have a dozen! Come back next year!

I decided to reply honestly. I said we didn't know yet, because this baby had a fatal heart condition and was expected to live only a few days after birth. We needed to take care of him first.

I realize this wasn't a typical answer, and people often don't know what to say when someone else is experiencing a tragedy. (A simple "I'm so sorry" is usually a good start.)

But I was even more taken aback when she replied coolly, "You must be a good Catholic."

Meaning what? That only Catholics would be unsophisticated enough to continue an obviously doomed pregnancy? Or was she dismissing my "fetus" as having no intrinsic value, only whatever superstitious, personal value that might be assigned to it by a Catholic? I was offended and probably should have torn up my check and walked out. But I really wanted that dress.

⟡

Our hospital had a perinatal-loss educator on staff, another indication of changing attitudes toward infant death. We were referred to her for help in preparing our birth plan.

Birth plans are a relatively new addition to the experience of childbirth. Not long ago, the "birth plan" involved going to the hospital and doing what the doctor told you to do. Parents obviously still have to allow for the unexpected, but writing a birth plan is a way of informing their caregivers of their preferences.

Friends generously shared their written birth plans with me, to help give us ideas.

At first it seemed overwhelmingly sad for us to write a birth plan for a birth that would end in death. We came to see it as a way of choreographing Gabriel's extraordinarily precious first few hours of life.

The perinatal-loss educator, who was also a nurse, met us in the hospital lobby one morning in late June. The first thing Annette did was give me a sympathetic hug. Of course I promptly fell apart.

She led us to the birth center and into one of the birthing rooms. The bed was freshly made, the sheets taut and clean, ready for some other mother-to-be. Mark and I sat on a couch, and Annette sat on a chair. "Would you like to tell me about your baby?" she asked.

We talked and talked, and all three of us cried. She told us about her own daughter, who had been stillborn several years earlier. She said her work helping bereaved parents was a way of honoring her own baby.

She also told us that of all the parents she had met, none regretted making the decision we had made. We assumed she was talking about comfort care.

No, she meant continuing the pregnancy. She said that some families who obtained abortions after receiving a devastating fatal diagnosis were at peace with their choice, while others regretted it deeply. But she said that all the parents she knew who continued their pregnancies were grateful for the time they had with their babies, however brief, even if the baby died before birth.

We honestly hadn't even thought of continuing the pregnancy as a decision. Carrying Gabriel until he was ready to be born was no more of a conscious choice for us than continuing to breathe.

She then showed us privately around the birth center, because we hadn't had a baby at that hospital before and certainly did not want to tour the center with a group of giddy expectant parents.

Finally, I asked to see the neonatal intensive care unit. I needed to see where other critically ill babies went, the place where we had decided not to send Gabriel.

It wasn't nearly as horrible as I expected. The lights were dim to protect premature infants' underdeveloped eyes, and the room was hushed except for the clicking and whooshing of the ventilators and other high-tech machines. A few medical workers walked quietly through the room, past the plastic hospital bassinets holding fragile newborns. We didn't venture past the doorway; it would have seemed almost sacrilegious to step any closer to someone else's sick baby.

I left relieved. Relieved that the NICU seemed to be a peaceful place for the babies who had been hospitalized that day, and relieved that Gabriel would not be going there.

◦⌒◦

The next morning was our "care conference," a meeting that included one of our perinatologists, our pediatric cardiologist, a neonatologist, and others, including Sandra, one of our favorite nurses. The point of the meeting was to inform everybody about our plans for when Gabriel arrived. His due date was only five weeks away.

We all settled in around a long conference table in the high-risk maternity center at the hospital. A staff member handed out copies of our birth plan.

Ours began: "Our overriding wish is that our son Gabriel's birth and short life be filled only with comfort and love."

We asked that Gabriel be placed on my chest immediately after birth, that Mark cut the umbilical cord, and that I breastfeed him as soon as possible. We wanted to give him his first bath together. We wanted to be with him at all times, including during the echocardiogram that was planned to confirm the diagnosis. We wanted Elena and Maria and other family members to see him as soon as possible. We planned to have our priest baptize Gabriel in the hospital room, with family and friends in attendance. We didn't want Gabriel to have any of the usual newborn shots, and of course we didn't want him to be circumcised. We wanted a sample of blood taken from his umbilical cord (a painless procedure) to be banked at the University of Minnesota in case genetic tests for HLHS were ever developed.

And, finally, we asked that Gabriel and I be discharged from the hospital early to maximize his time at home. "Thank you for helping us celebrate Gabriel's short life," we wrote.

We discussed a few other matters. The pregnancy and birth were not technically high risk, so we wanted to be treated as normally as possible. I wanted to labor and deliver in a birthing room; I wanted no part of getting wheeled down the hallway to a delivery room in front of strangers while in the throes of hard labor. It has always seemed to me that the doctor should come to the woman at that point, not the other way around. We wanted the actual moments of birth to be as peaceful as possible, with a minimal number of people in the room and no observers. Our regular pediatrician for the girls would be notified to care for Gabriel for as long as he did live.

I said that I did not want a C-section, but I would accept drugs to speed the contractions if doctors believed that it would make the difference between Gabriel being born alive or stillborn. "I want to hold him while he's alive," I said. I think I saw one of the doctors blinking back tears.

Someone was assigned to arrange hospice care once we brought Gabriel home from the hospital. It was possible that Gabriel might not survive that long, although babies with untreated HLHS tend to live for several days to a week. Our pediatric cardiologist gently cautioned that the moments leading up to Gabriel's death might be frightening for us.

I had made it through the whole meeting without crying, until then.

⁓

If anyone had come across my to-do list, it probably would have sounded awful: Diapers . . . cradle . . . clothes for burial . . . obituaries. At least the list gave us something to do, some small illusion of control. Each task gave us strange comfort, and we tried to do everything perfectly. All were ways of parenting Gabriel.

You can't come out yet, baby, because my to-do list isn't done.

Please don't come out yet, because I'm not ready to let you go.

⁓

We wanted Gabriel to be baptized. This wasn't because we believed that a few words would make the difference between our baby going to heaven and him going to limbo, a mercifully discredited idea. (Imagine the anguish of parents who may have believed that their unbaptized baby's

72

spirit was cast adrift into some amorphous mist.)
We wanted to give Gabriel a formal welcome into
a community of faith, a sacramental ritual that
has been used for generations before him and
will probably be used for generations after. I like
the description of a sacrament given by Andrew
Greeley and Mary Greeley Durkin: "A sacrament
is a created reality that discloses to us Uncreated
Reality. It is a sign of goodness, a hint of an explanation, an experience of otherness, a promise of
life, a touch of grace, a rumor of angels."[14] We
wanted Gabriel to be touched by that, for his sake
and for ours.

Anybody can baptize a baby, although a priest
usually performs the ritual. We were surprised to
learn that the Catholic Church has a special baptismal rite for dying babies. It is not last rites; it is
instead two sacraments at once, baptism and communion. The priest touches a communion host to
the baby's tongue and also administers a drop of
communion wine. Father Baer generously agreed
to come to the hospital to baptize Gabriel whenever
he was born.

We believed that even if Gabriel died before
being baptized, he would be—as a friend later wrote
eloquently—"in the immediate presence of God."

We also had to decide what to do with Gabriel's body after he died. Many people choose cremation for babies and keep the ashes in a tiny urn in their home. One company even makes small ceramic containers for the ashes of a baby, topped with a three-dimensional porcelain head of a sleeping cherub. They come in heartbreaking shades of pink and blue.

But we wanted to have a gravesite that the girls could visit if they wanted when they got older. It also seemed important that his brief life be marked with a headstone that would take several grown men to move and would stand as an enduring testament, bearing Gabriel's name through decades of snowfall and spring rains and sun.

Knowing that Gabriel would probably live only a few days after birth, when I still would be recuperating, we decided to make his burial arrangements before he was born. It was another way of parenting him.

We decided to bury him in my hometown of St. Joseph, about an hour away and in the heart of the central Minnesota area that inspired Garrison Keillor's fictional Lake Wobegon. My great-grandparents, grandparents, and other relatives on my dad's side are also buried nearby. And the funeral would be in the towering 1871 fieldstone church that was built by German-Catholic immigrants and includes rocks lugged from the farm of my great-grandfather Heinrich Küblbeck. Mark and I were married in that same church, as were my parents and my paternal grandparents.

Walking into a funeral home to make arrangements for a baby still kicking inside of me was going to be wrenching enough, so I spoke with one of the funeral directors a couple of times by telephone before we made the trip. I didn't know if I could get through telling the story from scratch once we got there. The funeral director was kind, and we made an appointment to come by.

The drive seemed interminable. How could the day be so beautiful and sunny, the freeway packed with people leaving for a Fourth of July weekend filled with parades and swimming and barbecues, when we were so sad?

We sat in our car in the parking lot of the funeral home for a moment, dreading going in. "Are you OK?" we asked each other. Let's get this over with.

The receptionist seemed surprised to see us. She said our funeral director had been called out on an emergency but she would try to find someone else to help us. The place was hushed, cool, and, well, funereal. A man in the requisite black suit soon walked into the reception area, in quiet conversation with another worker. The receptionist murmured something to him and motioned toward us.

We said hello, exchanged handshakes and pleas-antries, and then followed him downstairs. He was already partway down the stairs when he turned, nodding toward my eight-months-pregnant belly, and asked if I could handle the steps all right.

"I see you're expecting a happy occasion," he said brightly.

Nobody had told him.

"That's why we're here," Mark said.

I think the funeral director was so mortified at what he had said that he never regained his foot-ing during the rest of the meeting.

He led us to a windowless basement office, where we could discuss some of the ugliest aspects of death, such as embalming and price.

He offered to handle the obituary for us. We said we planned to place obituaries in the two metro-politan dailies where we lived as well as in the smaller local newspaper, and we said that it was important to us to write them ourselves.

The local newspaper didn't allow people to write obituaries, he told us. Because their listings were run at no charge, they had a formula: who, what, where, when, and a listing of survivors.

We thought that was a disservice to the families, even though the families might save a little money that way. Many people live their entire lives without ever getting their names in the paper, so printed obituaries can be an important commemoration of their lives and a keepsake for their families. Most metro-area dailies charge per line for obituary notices, but then the families are free to write eloquently about their loved ones, and many do.

We wanted a local obituary anyway, because Gabriel's wake, funeral, and burial were going to be held in the area. My hometown is still small enough that many people check the obituaries every day to see if someone has died to whom they need to pay their respects. My parents have run a small business in town for decades, a milk-delivery service that was owned by my grandfather and my great-grandfather before him, so they know a lot of people in town. There might be some people who would learn about Gabriel's death only through the newspaper and might want to come to the services, or at least send my parents a note of sympathy for the loss of their grandson. My parents would need support in their sorrow too.

Having talked about the obituary, it was time to shop for caskets. We followed the funeral director out of the office through a side door and into the windowless showroom. There was no point in trying not to cry. That horse was long since out of the barn. But I did try not to shake.

In the finest retail tradition, the most luxurious casket was displayed most prominently. Basking under spotlights near the entrance was the highly polished Presidential, its lid propped open for full appreciation of its pillowy satin interior.

The caskets all looked adult-sized. Where were the children's caskets? He led us to a closet and opened the door. Models of several styles were stored inside on shelves. Was the death of a child so rare, was our situation so freakish, that the merchandise could be stuffed away in a closet? Or were the miniature caskets hidden from view because they were too sad even for other grieving families to walk past?

At about eye level sat what appeared to be the Presidential Junior, glossy white with brass handles. It seemed as absurd to me as dressing a toddler in a formal white tux. It was slightly more than a thousand dollars. I've had cars that cost less than that.

The funeral director bent down to slide out the cheapest model, which was stored none too subtly on the bare floor. A thirty-five-dollar styrofoam box. I don't think so.

Like a morbid parody of Goldilocks and the Three Bears—too much, too little, just right—he then pulled the middle-of-the-line model off the shelf and set it on the floor at our feet. It was made out of white molded plastic, and if you rapped it with your knuckles it would probably sound like a picnic cooler. I recoiled. I was not going to bury our son in a picnic cooler.

Then he removed the lid and gently lifted the edges of the quilted white lining to show us the inside. There was a small ruffled pillow for the baby's head.

Oh, dear God. It looked like a bassinet.

I grabbed Mark's arm, and my cynicism dissolved into weeping.

❧

What I really wanted was for someone to make Gabriel's casket just for him. I had in mind the simple, handcrafted wooden coffins made by the Benedictine monks at the nearby Saint John's Abbey in Collegeville. All the monks, from the bread bakers to the most renowned of scholars, are laid to rest in those plain but dignified boxes of dark-stained pine harvested from the forests surrounding the monastery.

My father-in-law, Jack, is an expert woodworker who builds beautiful furniture and church altars (and dinosaur puzzles). Sparing us from broaching the idea to him ourselves, Mark's brother called Jack to suggest it and offered to fly from Cincinnati to Iowa to help. Jack immediately went to work in his sawdust-strewn basement workshop. He consulted with a funeral director friend for measurements, built a practice model, and sent photographs to us by e-mail. Then he carefully selected some planks of aromatic red cedar for what he has called one of the hardest things he has ever done.

꒳

It might seem pointless or even cruel to give someone a baby gift for a baby who is not going to live. But many parents of children who die ascribe great significance to tangible mementos that serve to acknowledge their baby's brief life. We were given a number of heartfelt gifts before Gabriel was even born.

My friend Gayla and her husband, Eric, both architects, spent an entire weekend designing and constructing a stunning stained-glass lamp for us. Each of its four rectangular panels has a distinct meaning: an abstract mother and child, surrounded by cut glass in celestial blue; a four-chambered heart, also designed to represent Mark's heart joined with mine; an abstract image of a pregnant woman, signifying Gabriel safe inside of me; and a milky-white heart that also resembles an angel's wings at rest. After making many drafts and finally settling on a design, they were astonished to see that running unintentionally throughout the panels were images of a fish and a cross—two symbols of Christianity. Their inspired work of art is beautiful on so many levels.

My sister Karen gave me a bottle of water from
Lourdes. Our friend JoAnn, who had cared for
Elena when she was a baby, knit Gabriel a blue
sweater and booties.

At the end of my sister Stacy's baby shower,
she took me aside and said she had something
for me too. Inside the gift-wrapping was a soft
cotton newborn gown and cap. Gabriel should
have something new to come home in, she said. I
had been able to put up a brave face at the shower
until then.

And from my mom came a baby blanket, of
the kind she sews for each new grandchild. She
had already bought some fabric before Gabriel's
heart condition was diagnosed, but she set it
aside and searched for a fabric with angels on
it instead—no small feat in May. All she could
find were inappropriate Christmas remnants,
so she finally explained to the store clerks what
she was looking for and why. The clerks ended
up crying with her and helped her find just the
right fabric, a cream-colored cloth with a pattern
of little angels in blue and red blowing trumpets
of gold.

She gave it to me on Mother's Day.

We treasure all of these things.

❧

One way we decided to honor and celebrate the experience of waiting with Gabriel was to have a sitting with a professional photographer while I was still pregnant. My friend Gayla told me about a St. Paul photographer whose unique specialty was taking elegant, tasteful black and-white portraits of bare-bellied pregnant women and of newborns.

I called the photographer and left a message explaining our circumstances. I also asked if she would consider coming to our home to photograph Gabriel during the first day or two after he was born, before his heart would start to fail. We wanted as many pictures as possible, but we wouldn't be able to bring him to her studio.

Claudia called back and said of course, she would accommodate us in whatever way she could. She sounded genuinely empathetic, and I liked her even over the telephone.

I was eager for the sitting, because for once since getting Gabriel's diagnosis it felt as if we were doing something to truly celebrate the pregnancy itself.

On a steamy July afternoon, we stepped out of our sandals and into Claudia's refreshing living room studio, feeling the cool hardwood floor under our bare feet. Even the colors were cool and calming, gauzy white and baby blue. White fabric backdrops were draped across part of the room, diffusing the afternoon light. Sepia and black-and-white prints of pregnant women, nursing mothers, and newborns lined one wall.

Claudia talked with us about some of her prints, pointing out lighting that she particularly liked, or a position of a hand, or a baby's rosebud mouth. She laughed as she told us that some of her relatives wished she'd do something more "respectable," such as photographing high school seniors sitting in wicker chairs. But she said she loved her work and loved the idea that she was helping commemorate the journey of pregnancy.

Our culture is ambivalent about hugely pregnant women; even some of Claudia's clients weren't quite comfortable with the idea of growing along with their baby. Some wanted to come in for a sitting when they were only four or five months pregnant, before they got "too big." (Claudia said photographing at that stage mostly makes them look as though they ate too much for breakfast.) She preferred photographing women about two weeks before their due date, when she said the shape of the belly was at its fullest and most beautiful.

We talked about Gabriel. She said how sorry she was and that she felt honored to help us honor him.

She draped me strategically with yards of white tulle, checked the lighting, and started shooting. You'd think I would have felt completely ridiculous. But it was all done in such a spirit of joy, of commemoration. We were creating a beautiful and tangible record of my time carrying Gabriel. It didn't feel ridiculous. It felt sacred.

She was just finishing when she asked if we had any last ideas. I suggested trying one more, of just my bare stomach with both Mark's hand and mine resting on it, our wedding rings visible. That was a pose she hadn't used with other clients before, so we experimented a little, hands resting this way, fingers angled a bit that way.

That last shot is one of my most treasured pictures of Gabriel, even though you can't see him at all because he was still cradled safely inside of me.

❦

Gabriel also would need something to be buried in.

I wanted to keep every piece of clothing that touched his skin while he was alive, so I wanted something brand-new for his burial, and I wanted it to be white.

Dreading this shopping trip, we procrastinated as long as we could. Because we wanted it to be a family affair, we brought the girls and promised them ice cream afterward. We went to the infants' section at an expensive department store, where we rarely bought children's clothes because kids grow out of them so fast. We settled on a soft white cotton hooded jacket with buttons in the front and a little pair of matching elastic-waist pants.

We brought the outfit to the register and then realized that he would need something on his feet too. Mark went back and picked out a pair of soft white knit booties. We were the only shoppers in the department, but the clerk rang up our purchase without saying a word.

Please say something. Ask me if this is for my baby's baptism so I can tell you it's for my baby's funeral.

"Have a nice day," she said.

❧

It was more anguishing in some ways to prepare for Gabriel's time at home than to handle the logistics of his death.

Jack had made a family cradle out of Iowa catalpa before the first Neuzil grandchild was born. Both Elena and Maria slept in it as newborns, as have a number of cousins. Each time a baby grows out of it, the parents write the baby's name on the bottom of the cradle, along with the dates that the baby slept in it. Then they disassemble it and pack it to be shipped for the next arrival. I wanted Gabriel to lie in that cradle, at least briefly, although we expected that he would spend most of his life in someone's arms. So it was shipped to us a couple of weeks before his due date. Elena begged us daily to take it out of the box and put it together for Gabriel. But because there was a small chance he might not live long enough to come home, we left the cradle untouched in its long cardboard box, leaning against a wall in our dining room. We planned to dispatch somebody to put it together for us when it came time to bring Gabriel home.

I also daydreamed about nursing Gabriel in our pine-floored enclosed porch, sunlight filtering through the sheer ivory curtains patterned with flowers and vines, a fabric called Tree of Life. We had told family and friends that we wanted people to meet Gabriel while he was still alive, and I pictured people sitting in that sunroom with us, admiring our beautiful baby while he nursed and slept.

We would also need some diapers and other essentials. I didn't want to buy those ahead of time. I worried irrationally that I might jinx things, that somehow he might die at the hospital if I dared go to the baby aisle at Target. So I gave my sister Stacy a short list of items to bring to the house when we brought Gabriel home: newborn diapers, a travel-sized bottle of Baby Magic baby bath—I figured the travel size would last his whole life—and a new baby washcloth and towel. I pictured laying him on plush towels on the large counter in our master bathroom and bathing him as the afternoon sun slanted through the blinds. I couldn't wait to look into his eyes and rub soap over his soft skin with my bare hands.

༄

Everything was ready. My hospital bag was packed with the usual items, including Gabriel's going-home outfit from Stacy and extra film for the camera. It also held some more poignant items: a delicate baptismal gown once worn by my mother as well as by Elena and Maria, the Lourdes water from Karen, and a plaster-of-Paris footprint kit that I threw in as an afterthought, just in case he couldn't come home. All our preparations had been made for Gabriel's birth—and for his death.

His due date no longer loomed like an execution date. You'd think we would have awakened each day feeling like throwing up, not knowing if we would remember this day always as the day he was born or as the day he died. Instead we were on high alert, our senses heightened, feeling bizarrely and intensely alive. Maybe that had something to do with all those people praying for us, which was a good thing, because I really couldn't pray myself. Maybe it was tightly controlled panic. But when my sisters would call each day, inquiring about contractions, I would describe myself as feeling strangely serene. I was concentrating not on Gabriel's imminent death but on his imminent birth.

That is, until several days of false labor that began on his due date. *What is going on? Is he going to be born today or not?* We finally went in for an exam at the birth center, where my contractions stopped. We listened on the monitor to Gabriel's heart continuing to beat steadily.

The sight of the birth center's preparations hit me with an almost physical force. A little blue knit cap was draped over the side of a plastic bassinet, and an oxygen canister—usually hidden away unless needed—sat ready. Posted outside my door was a discreet picture, of the kind that I knew hospitals used to indicate a sad situation inside. It was a photograph of a green leaf with a single raindrop on it.

Strangers too were preparing for the birth and death of our baby.

❧

The nurse kindly sent us back home. Soon, maybe tomorrow, a Sunday. That would be a good day. Counting the days ahead, I wondered when his funeral would be.

More important, I wondered what he looked like and what his days would be like with us at home. Does he look like his sisters? Does he have blue-green eyes like Elena and me or brown eyes like Mark and Maria? What will he sound like when he cries? I yearned to feel his soft cheek against mine, to feel his swaddled weight against my chest, to cup the back of his head in my hand, to breathe deeply of his sweet baby smell. To try to imprint everything of him on my memory forever.

I was ready to meet my son.

Chapter 4

hello

"IT'S GOING TO BE A meteorologically perfect day," the radio announcer said as we lay in our bed on that August Sunday morning. Clear skies, a light breeze, a break in the sweltering humidity. One of those summer days when the heat lifts and you notice once again the subtle shades of green in the gardens and lawns and in the leaves fluttering in relief against the celestial blue sky.

It soon became clear that this would also be Gabriel's birthday.

We thought going to Mass might help calm us, so there we sat, on the uncomfortably hard pews, me checking my watch every fifteen minutes and then every ten and finally whispering to Mark that I couldn't sit during the contractions anymore. We stood in the back for the last few minutes of the service, which also would give us first crack at the new priest when he exited the church. We hadn't met him yet and thought we would briefly introduce ourselves, just in case we couldn't reach Father Baer when it came time for Gabriel's baptism.

Mass ended and the priest walked past us and out into the sunshine. We followed, only to see him keep going down the sidewalk and around the corner, his vestments billowing in the breeze. It happened to be the one Sunday he wouldn't be greeting parishioners on the front steps, because of an ice cream social in his honor to be held on the church lawn in just a few minutes. *Oh well,* we thought; Gabriel would probably live a few days, so we'd have time to find someone. We shrugged and walked home.

"How's it going?" someone asked along the way, a woman who knew only that our baby was probably going to be very sick.

"Every ten minutes," I said. She wished us luck.

We had a quick lunch at home and called some friends to watch the girls. I set aside matching sundresses for them to wear later when they came to the hospital for Gabriel's baptism. We called our parents and also the birth center to say we were coming. Unlike the day before, the floor was nearly full, and the nurse said they might have to put me somewhere else. I asked her if she had seen our birth plan—she had—and I said it was *very* important to us to be in a regular birthing room. She said she'd try.

It was high time to be getting to the hospital. Mark took our usual route down Grand Avenue, past florists and trendy cafés and chic baby stores. Gripped by contractions, I wondered wildly if Summit Avenue would have been faster.

Our nurse from the previous day, Susan, met us once we arrived on the maternity floor and put her arm around my shoulder.

"It's for real today?" she asked.

Yes.

She led us to a regular birthing room, just as we had requested. She said she was with another patient but would switch so she could be with us. Already posted on the door outside our room was the photograph of a leaf with a single raindrop.

❧

Our family and friends started to trickle into the private waiting room that had been set aside for them. There were my parents; my sister Karen, her husband, Tracy, and their baby, Jesse; my sister Jane and her husband, Brian; my pregnant sister, Stacy, and her husband, Bob; my sister Molly and her husband, Tim; and our friend Barb. Mark's parents were on their way, driving from Iowa.

Tell me again who's here, I'd say to Mark as another contraction hit.

༄

I had been virtually unmedicated during my last delivery, which was assisted by a nurse-midwife. It was painful and exhausting, of course, but immediately after the birth I was suffused with feelings of power and exhilaration. I remember taking pictures of Mark bathing Maria just minutes after she was born, all the adults laughing and smiling, and me actually saying to Mark, "I could do that again." I was hoping that Gabriel's birth could be like that too, or at least that my awareness wouldn't be clouded by drugs.

I forgot about the possibility of back labor. Big mistake.

Every labor is different, as anyone who's given birth more than once knows. The intensity of the pain varies from woman to woman, and even from pregnancy to pregnancy, depending on variables that include the baby's position and size and the mother's fatigue and emotional state. And then there's back labor, caused by the baby descending in the "stargazing" position, face up, with the back of the head toward the woman's spine. A typical labor is to back labor what an ordinary headache is to a raging, behind-the-eyeballs migraine. It is like an unrelenting steamroller moving from the inside out. It is not the labor pain that the childbirth books refer to gingerly as "discomfort."

(I have resolved that if I am *ever* in that kind of physical pain again, I will roar like a madwoman until anesthesiologists from all around the hospital drop whatever they're doing, midsurgery or mid-sandwich, and come running to *shut that woman up*.)

The nurses tried—and tried, and tried—to place an IV so I could get an epidural. It took three nurses and a full hour to place the IV, but no anesthesiologists were available, and soon it was too late.

~

"You're going to have a baby," our perinatologist says, her voice calm and controlled.

In a choreographed blur, the foot of the bed drops, instruments appear, drapes go up, masks go on, time simultaneously races and stops altogether. *Push.*

My sister Stacy, walking in the hallway at that exact moment, sees a team of doctors rushing into my room. What she hears coming out of the open door is a cry of such anguish that she thinks Gabriel is already dead.

The labor nurse puts her face inches away from mine. "Use that," she commands firmly. "Use that to push your baby out."

One more push. A tremendous, searing, unstoppable rush. At 4:42 P.M., Gabriel is born.

Gabriel is born!

He is on my chest, crying weakly, wet and warm and *alive.*

"Hello, Gabriel, I'm your mommy," I say into his ear. "I'm so glad you're here."

Mark cuts the umbilical cord, and the neonatology team sweeps Gabriel to the nearby warmer to try to suction the meconium—too, too much—from his lungs.

Breathe, sweetheart. Cough that up.

"Do you want us to give him a puff of oxygen so he can say hello to you?" the labor nurse asks. Yes, yes, of course. I can't see what they're doing—the warmer is surrounded by people in blue scrubs—but I hear him gagging a little from the suctioning and trying to cry.

They suction all they can. His crying still sounds as if his lungs are disturbingly congested, as if he needs to cough forcefully but doesn't have the strength to do so. After five minutes his Apgar score is a nine out of ten anyway, the score of a perfectly healthy baby.

"Don't you want us to do anything else?" someone on the neonatology team asks.

For a microsecond, my thoughts leap. *Is there
something else? Some new treatment we don't know about?*

We shake our heads no.

℘

At last we are holding our beautiful baby.

Swaddled in his hospital blanket decorated with
pastel teddy bears and hot-air balloons, he is crying
with some effort, his eyes squeezed tightly closed. He
has the plump newborn cheeks his sisters had and a
hint of downy dark hair. He is a little pale, and his
fingernails are faintly blue. He is beautiful. We are
overwhelmed with pride and love—and concern—for
the newest member of our family.

Mark helps unwrap him for the measurements—
seven pounds, nine ounces, twenty-two inches long.
Gabriel does not like this one bit. He wails, his
mouth wide open in protest. Then he is swaddled
again, an off-white knit cap warming his head, and
placed in my arms. He settles down and falls asleep.

It's time to show off our new son!

The waiting room empties into our room. There
are tears and smiles and camera flashes. Karen teases
me that it's not fair that my babies are born already

looking like Gerber babies. He *is* beautiful, cream-skinned and perfect and plump, with no bruises or misshapen head from the delivery. My parents hold him briefly.

The pediatric cardiologist on call and the echocardiogram technician arrive, wheeling the machine into the room so I can be present for the exam. We invite my parents to stay.

As the cardiologist readies Gabriel for the exam, Mom and Dad give me a baptism gift, a gold necklace pendant of a mother and child. Mom helps me put it on.

The exam gets under way. His knit cap is starting to slip off; watching from my bed I ask Mom to put it back on. She does, then stays by his bassinet, stroking his head.

The pediatric cardiologist says it most definitely is hypoplastic left heart syndrome, pointing on the screen to the empty shadow where the left ventricle should be. It is among the severest cases she has seen.

We ask if the exam gives any indication of how long he will live. No, she says; he could live for up to two weeks. My mom starts mentally calculating how to schedule people in shifts to help us at home for that long.

The exam is finished, and Gabriel is once again in my arms, the sweet heft of my sleeping baby.

We decide to baptize him at 8:00 that evening. Barb has been paging Father Baer but hasn't been able to reach him. The hospital's Catholic chaplain is off-duty tonight, so Barb will keep trying to call our priest.

It's dinnertime, so we urge my parents to make sure everybody gets something to eat, telling them about an Italian deli nearby. See you in a while.

It is just the three of us now, Mark and me and our son. Mark makes a brief long-distance call from the bedside phone to tell his brother that Gabriel has arrived.

I kiss Gabriel's forehead. It is cool.

The nurse comes back and checks his temperature and his heart. His heart rate is only 67 beats per minute, much slower than the normal newborn rate of 100 to 120 beats a minute. She slips out of the room.

I kiss him again and whisper to him, "Don't leave yet."

Mark finishes his conversation and hangs up the phone. I tell him that the nurse seemed concerned about Gabriel's heart rate. She comes back and listens with her stethoscope again.

"Six," she said.

Six? We don't understand.

Her face close to mine, she says gently, "Your baby is dying."

No! Not yet!

The words scream through my mind, but nothing comes out except a sob.

❧

"My family's leaving!" I cry a moment later. The nurse leaves the room and then breaks into a run. She finds Barb, who has just returned with bags of sandwiches, in the hallway outside the waiting room.

Everyone is still there.

"Are you with Amy's family?" the nurse asks. Barb says she is.

The nurse says, "You all need to get in there, *now.*"

"Is he going?" Barb asks.

"Yes."

❧

Everybody streams into the room. All our faces are wet with tears.

"I thought we were going to be able to keep him longer," I say helplessly. I wanted the girls to hold him. I wanted to nurse him. I wanted to bring him home.

Someone mentions the priest.

"You don't have time," the nurse says urgently. "You realize that anybody can baptize a baby, right?"

Yes, we know. She offers to get some tap water from the bathroom sink. Mark rummages in my hospital bag instead for the bottle of water from Lourdes. Our tears would have been more than enough. He touches Gabriel's forehead with a drop of water, making the sign of the cross.

"I baptize you in the name of the Father, the Son, and the Holy Spirit," he says, his voice thick with crying.

Gabriel is in my lap. Mark and I are cradling his head and his cheek, and Mark's arm is around me. Gabriel's eyes are closed. He appears to be sleeping peacefully. *Oh, sweetheart, I never even saw your eyes.* "Let's look at him," I whisper. We open the blanket and see his arms resting on his chest, his knees pulled up as though he were still in the womb, those tiny feet that kicked me for months. Everything about him seems perfect.

We wrap him up again. My hands cradle his bare head and cup his shoulder. Mark holds Gabriel's left hand, and Gabriel's fingers grip Mark's little finger.

We are surrounded by people who love him.

Like holding a vigil for a baby about to be born, all of us simply wait together, waiting with Gabriel.

The only sounds are of people crying softly. Gabriel is in the same bed where he had been born, the sheets still bloodstained from his birth. We watch as he takes small, infrequent breaths, and finally his imperfect little heart stops beating altogether.

Gabriel relaxes his hold on Mark's finger. Mark looks at the clock. It is 7:10 P.M., two and a half hours since Gabriel's first breath.

❧

A moment later, we heard the curtain in the room being pulled aside, the metal curtain rings sliding across the metal rod.

My brother-in-law Tracy stepped into the room and said, "I have the archbishop with me."

You have *who*?

While Barb had been trying in vain to reach our priest, Tracy looked out of a window in the waiting room and saw the Cathedral of St. Paul and its tarnished green copper dome looming in the distance. He asked if anybody thought Mark and I would mind if another priest performed the baptism. Without saying where he was going, he left, found his car in the parking garage, and drove to the cathedral. Now he was back, along with Archbishop Harry Flynn, the spiritual leader of the 760,000-member Archdiocese of St. Paul and Minneapolis.

"We already did it," somebody blurted.

"We think he's already gone," I said.

He approached the bed and reverently cradled Gabriel's head in his hands.

"Gabriel is with God now," he said.

༄

Archbishop Flynn later wrote this in his newspaper column:

On a late Sunday afternoon in August, I was sitting on the patio that looks out over the city of St. Paul. Actually, I was reading the Sunday newspapers.

Sister Maria, one of the sisters who takes care of my residence, came out to me and told me that there was a man at the front door speaking about a baby who was very ill and needed to be baptized.

I went to the front door. . . . They wanted a priest to baptize the child. Would I come?

Of course I would come. To go to the hospital and be with those parents would be a great privilege for me, a priest.

I went in and got dressed and then was driven to the Children's Hospital in St. Paul. The gentleman who came to my door brought me to the room, and the scene will be seared in my mind and in my heart for as long as I live.

There was the mother on the bed holding and cradling her child. The child had died. The father had his arms around the mother and the child—cradling both of them. They were crying . . .

I touched the child, who seemed to me to be sleeping. He was warm and beautiful.

I said to the father, "Not only have you given that child natural life, but through the waters of baptism you have given that child an eternal life in Christ."[1]

༄

The archbishop prayed over Gabriel, then over Mark and me and everyone else in the room. His voice was hushed, calming, comforting. The room seemed bathed in a presence of overwhelming love. As several people described it later, it seemed as though more people were in the room with us. It felt holy, as though a veil had momentarily parted and we could feel the spirit of God.

༄

The archbishop had barely left when our friend David brought in Elena and Maria, dressed in their sundresses for Gabriel's baptism.

They rushed into the room excitedly, telling us about the toys they had played with that afternoon and the pizza they had eaten for supper. Everyone else slipped out to let us introduce the girls to their baby brother.

We explained that his body had already stopped working but that they could touch him if they wanted. They did, curious, still chatting happily.

A young doctor came in to confirm Gabriel's death. We explained to Elena and Maria that they needed to be very quiet while the doctor listened to Gabriel's heart with a stethoscope, because he needed to check that it wasn't working anymore. He listened.

"I'm sorry," he said. We nodded, and he left.

Barb came in and escorted the girls out to get some cookies at the nurses' station so I could take a bath and somebody could change the sheets. Getting out of bed was surreal; the last time I had been on my feet, I was still pregnant, and now Gabriel was already dead.

❧

We asked that the girls be brought back into the room for Gabriel's bath.

First we took pictures of the big sisters each holding their baby brother. Elena was big enough to hold him in her lap, supporting his head with her arm like an expert. She spontaneously leaned down to kiss his head, her blond hair brushing against his dark wisps. Maria held him with the help of a pillow.

A new nurse, Cindy, prepared Gabriel's warm bath. She laid him on heated white towels and put some bath lotion and water on my hands, telling me to work up a good lather. I smoothed the fragrant bubbles over the baby-soft skin of Gabriel's chest, his shoulders, and his tiny fingers, perfect and limp. I can feel it in my mind still.

I washed his face with a warm washcloth, instinctively keeping the soap out of his closed eyes. Then Mark took over, washing Gabriel's back and adorable bottom with his bare hands.

We dried him with more warm towels and laid him on the angel blanket from my mom, which we had spread out over the fresh sheets on my bed. Maria decided to touch his feet, her pudgy toddler hands tentatively exploring his toes. We dressed him in the soft cotton going-home outfit from Stacy and swaddled him in the angel blanket.

Barb took a family photo: me holding Gabriel, Elena standing next to me on one side of the rocking chair, and Mark on the other, one arm around Maria.

We invited everyone back in. As the sun set, his grandparents and aunts and uncles and dear friend took turns sitting in the rocking chair and holding

him, stroking his cheek and gazing at his face with
sorrow and love.

❧

All this time, Mark's parents had been making their
anxious five-hour drive from Iowa, with Gabriel's
casket in the back of their minivan. They had been
worried for months that they might not arrive in time
to see Gabriel alive. We always reassured them that he
probably would live for at least a couple of days.

They arrived at the hospital and walked up to the
front desk to ask where my room was. The receptionist tapped a few keys on her computer. Without
even making eye contact, she chewed her gum and
announced casually, while strangers milled about in
the lobby, "The baby's already dead."

That was how they learned of the death of their
grandson.

❧

Late into the night, people continued to come as
soon as they could get to the hospital: another of
my sisters, Paula, and her husband, Mike; Barb's

husband, Gene; and later Father Baer, who had been out of town. So many wonderful people came to meet Gabriel.

❧

Our night nurse, Cindy, encouraged us to take Gabriel's footprints before we went to sleep. She tenderly made several prints of his feet and his hands, and she helped us mix the plaster of Paris that we had brought along for a permanent imprint of his feet. While Mark held him, she carefully snipped a tiny lock of almost-black hair from the back of Gabriel's head.

Then she helped us swaddle him snugly and laid him in his plastic bassinet between my bed and Mark's foldout chair.

Physically and emotionally exhausted, we turned out the lights and tried to rest. Much tossing and turning later, my mind racing but desperate for sleep, I pressed the call button and asked whether the effects of a sleeping pill would carry over until morning. I wanted to be alert the next day. The nurse said the pill would wear off by the morning, so I asked for one and took it.

❧

The sleeping pill lasted only a couple of hours. Awake again, I lay on my side, gazing tearfully at Gabriel. Then the thought came to me:

Why is my baby in that bassinet all alone?

So in the dim fluorescent light, I rearranged the pillows on my bed to make a place for him. I carefully lifted him out of the bassinet and gently laid him next to me. My arm draped over his chest, my cheek touching his cool forehead, I fell asleep with my son for one last time.

Chapter 5

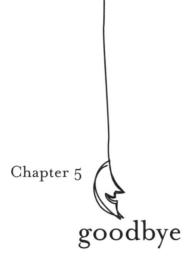

goodbye

MORNING DAWNED OVERCAST as raindrops trickled like tears down the windowpane.

I caressed Gabriel's face on the pillow next to mine and kissed his forehead again, by now ice cold. *Oh, sweetheart, you're really gone.*

Mark and I took turns holding him and rocking him in the rocking chair. We finally called the nurses' station to say that we were ready for someone to take him away. A nurse helped us change his clothes, dressing him in one of the hospital's baby gowns so we could take his going-home outfit with us, still fragrant from the bath and from him.

We laid him in a hospital blanket in the nurse's arms. Then she took another blanket and draped it completely over him, covering even his face. For a moment I didn't understand. Why was she covering our beautiful baby? Then came the awful realization that she needed to hide him from people outside our room. Our beautiful, dead baby.

She walked past the curtain and out the door, taking with her our baby and a part of us.

❧

A few minutes later the girls' pediatrician came to see us, even though she knew Gabriel had already died. She was crying even before she walked into the room.

❧

There was no reason for us to stay. We asked to be sent home.

The doctor on duty, who would have delivered Gabriel had our perinatologist not come in for us on her day off, stepped partway into our room with a resident and stood awkwardly by the curtain.

"I'm sorry about your situation," the doctor said mildly, as though we had just lost a wallet.

We didn't have a "situation"; we had a son. Say "baby." Say his name.

He proceeded to ask a few perfunctory questions about my physical state before clearing me to be discharged from the hospital. That was it.

To this day, Mark regrets not pulling himself to his full six-foot-three-inch height, directing his attention to the resident, and saying something like, *Do you realize what you just saw? Don't ever behave like that with your patients. You have a chance to do better.*

⁓

When we got home late that morning the cardboard box containing the cradle was gone, mailed off to Cincinnati for the next baby. On the dining room table was a vase with a dozen roses, eleven red and one white.

The girls were back home too, being watched by Mark's parents. How we needed to see our girls! Mark and I were terribly dazed, but still we noticed how sad Elena was that Gabriel didn't come home and sleep in the cradle. She kept saying that he didn't sleep in the cradle.

Although she was not quite two and a half, Maria understood some of what was happening too. As I tucked her into bed that night, she looked up at me with her beautiful big brown eyes and said,

"But Gabriel didn't even have any cookies."

❧

That first night without Gabriel, I had the most vivid dream. I was kneeling on the floor and leaning over Mark, trying to comfort him, when suddenly I found that I was leaning over Gabriel, his pale little hands resting on his chest just as they had when he died. He opened his eyes. They were a gorgeous, translucent blue. "I love you," I said, crying.

He said, "I love you too."

❧

Mark also had a vivid dream. He was pushing Gabriel in a stroller through unfamiliar terrain that became increasingly treacherous and muddy. He knew he had to keep pushing him, but the mud was terribly deep. He made it through to the other side, but Gabriel had mud all over him and was having trouble breathing. Mark bent down and cleaned everything off Gabriel's face until he could breathe freely again. Gabriel's daddy took care of him, and then Gabriel was fine.

∽

We had intentionally left some details of the funeral unplanned, feeling that we should reserve a few things until after Gabriel died. We hadn't expected that we would have to plan the rest of it so soon after his birth.

We chose this passage from the Gospel of Luke: "Let the little children come to me, and do not hinder them, for the kingdom of God belongs to such as these."

I needed meaningful music for the service but could hardly think straight. Our talented musician friends Joe and Cathy agreed to play piano and sing and made wonderful suggestions.

I had saved Elena's drawing of our family all these months, the picture of a mom and a dad and three children that she had drawn on the day of Gabriel's diagnosis. That became the front cover for Gabriel's funeral program. On the back cover, my sister Paula photocopied his footprints.

Our friends Steve and Mary, who were all too familiar with the pain of losing a child because their son Steven had died after four and a half months of pregnancy just a few years before, scoured several gift shops until they found a medal of the archangel Gabriel. Mark had asked them to buy two: one for him to wear on a chain around his neck and the other to bury with Gabriel.

I carefully took Gabriel's burial clothes off the hangers, snipped off the price tags, and took the soft cotton booties out of their plastic bag. I had forgotten that he would need a little T-shirt with snaps at the bottom to wear under his outfit, so I rummaged in a closet for a box of newborn hand-me-downs from Elena and Maria. I chose one that had been worn by both his sisters, its pastel blue bunnies slightly faded from washings.

Our friend Melissa had crocheted a blanket for Gabriel, just as she had done for each of our girls. At the last minute I was possessed by the thought that the casket might be too big and we'd need to put a blanket in it with Gabriel. Melissa hadn't given us the blanket yet, so she sent it by courier to make sure it would arrive at our home in time for the funeral. It was beautiful, made of lavender and pink and white yarn.

The funeral home was handling the formulaic obituary to be placed in the local daily newspaper. For the Minneapolis and St. Paul newspapers, we put the finishing touches on our own obituary and faxed it in.

It began: "Baby Gabriel Kuebelbeck Neuzil, 2½ hours old and perfect except for his heart. . . . In his short life, he knew only love."

❧

One of the funeral directors called. He said he was very sorry, but the local newspaper was refusing to print Gabriel's obituary.

You see, even though the funeral was going to be held locally, the cemetery was local, and Gabriel's little body was at that very moment at a local funeral home, his death wasn't local enough. They ran obituaries only for current or former residents of the area. I had lived there, but Gabriel hadn't. I didn't have the energy to scream. Gabriel didn't have time to be a resident of *anywhere!*

Somebody at the newspaper told the funeral director that if we really wanted a notice published, we could take out a classified ad in a different section of the paper. A classified ad! Nobody looks in the classifieds for funeral notices. They look in the obituaries. What were we supposed to do, place an ad in the personals section, next to "DIVORCE: $99"? Or somewhere between Autos and Garage Sales, maybe under *D* for *Dead*? We were trying so hard to honor Gabriel's life, including notifying people about his funeral, and now an illogical policy was keeping his funeral notice out of the paper.

Although my instinct was to call a top editor at the paper and unleash my postpartum hormones and grief and rage into his ear, we thought better of it. We enlisted a journalist colleague to intercede for us, to no avail. We were told secondhand that the newspaper simply couldn't accommodate this unanticipated situation on such short notice. Never mind that handling the unexpected is something that any good newspaper is supposed to be able to do.

The newspaper's refusal resulted in some people missing our baby's funeral.

❧

Pictures of any newborn are precious; our photographs of Gabriel are priceless to us. We told people before he was born that we wanted as many pictures of him as possible, even if what was happening at the time seemed too sad. Especially considering that many bereaved parents have only one fading hospital Polaroid of their child, if that, we feel blessed to have nearly 150 photographs documenting Gabriel's short life.

One stunning shot was taken by a nursing assistant moments after he was born. He is under warming lights in a bassinet, bathed in a golden glow. Visible are the gloved hands of a neonatologist, listening with a stethoscope to Gabriel's heart. Gabriel is crying and so clearly alive.

Whoever that nursing assistant was, thank you.

❧

We spent the night before the funeral at my parents' home in St. Joseph, where we saw for the first time the many pictures my mom had taken of Gabriel. She has always had an eye for photography and has recorded every family event, and I am grateful that she had the presence of mind to keep taking pictures of Gabriel even through her tears.

My dad had a vivid dream about Gabriel too. In the dream, Gabriel told him that he loved swinging on the swings in our backyard, on the swing set Mark and my dad had built. Gabriel also said he liked the baseball game, my dad told me, sounding puzzled. Gabriel said he liked the baseball game.

I asked, "You know that we took him to a baseball game, right?"

No, he didn't know.

❧

My mind knew Gabriel was dead, but my body didn't. Like clockwork, my milk came in. It seemed like a cruel twist of nature for this perfect nutrition to well up for my baby on the day of his funeral. Don't ever tell a woman whose baby has just died that God must have needed another baby in heaven. God cannot possibly need a baby more than a mother whose very body is weeping for her child.

❧

We rushed around on the morning of the funeral, trying to get the girls ready on time. *We can't be late for our own baby's funeral.* I was strangely eager for the wake; I could hardly wait to see Gabriel again and to hold him. We had already told the funeral director that we wanted to hold him once more before closing the casket.

My parents drove us to the funeral home, the same place where we had let the girls gently touch my Grandma Kuebelbeck's body in her casket. I was crying even before we walked in the door.

Waiting in the lobby for us, with hugs and more tears, was the rest of our families. One of my sisters noticed that even the funeral director standing in the corner had tears in his eyes. (We learned later that they only handle about one child's funeral a year.)

Then it was time for Mark and me to see Gabriel privately. The funeral director led us into a hushed, carpeted, darkly paneled room. Gabriel's casket sat on a small table at the far end of the room, dwarfed by a bouquet of peach roses and daisies. The red cedar of the casket had been sanded and varnished with care, its corners meticulously squared. Along one side of the casket lay a small black-walnut cross also made by Mark's dad, identical to those he had made for their home church in Iowa. On another side lay a blue knit cap from the hospital, just like the one that had been draped over the hospital bassinet on the day before his birth. Visible from across the room was the profile of Gabriel's forehead and his perfect little nose.

We approached, nervous and tearful.

"Oh, sweetheart," I whispered.

Mark carefully slipped the chain with the medal of the archangel Gabriel over Gabriel's head, arranging the medal on his son's chest.

We didn't need to bury the handmade blanket with him after all; the twenty-four-inch-long casket was just the right size. We displayed the blanket near the casket instead. I was grateful to have another memento of him to keep. That golden-hued photograph of Gabriel newly born stood in a frame on a table nearby, next to a vase of white roses and baby's breath.

Elena and Maria were allowed in next. They stood on a stool in front of the casket, and we let them touch his clothing and his hands and the white booties on his feet.

Then came his grandparents, aunts, uncles, cousins, and friends, and later came more friends, extended relatives, neighbors, and coworkers.

Too soon it was time to move to the church for the funeral. Father Baer led the group in a few words of prayer, and everyone went on ahead to the church while Mark and I stayed behind.

At last, the moment I'd been waiting for, my chance to hold Gabriel one final time. Barb asked if we wanted her to stay to take a picture. Yes, please. Mark sat next to me as the funeral director carefully placed Gabriel's body in the angel blanket draped over my arms and lap.

I knew that I needed to hold his body again. I am forever grateful that I did, but not for the reasons I expected. Holding his body gave me final, irrefutable proof that Gabriel was no longer in that shell. It felt like a doll, stiff and hollow and light. It didn't smell like him. It didn't even really look like him. It *wasn't* him. He didn't need it anymore, so we didn't either.

It might seem counterintuitive, but holding that empty body for just a few moments made it much easier to release it and to close the red cedar lid of that small casket forever.

❧

A police officer on a motorcycle escorted the funeral procession along the two-block drive to the church. Mark thought the police escort seemed excessive in a town that didn't even have a stoplight on its main street, but I was grateful for it. *Stop what you're doing, everybody, and wait for us to drive past. My baby is dead.*

We pulled up to the fieldstone church behind the white funeral-home minivan carrying Gabriel's casket. I don't know why they didn't use a hearse. In a funny way it's appropriate that our baby rode in one of those ubiquitous minivans at least once.

As is the local tradition, family and extended family were waiting outside to follow us and Gabriel's casket into the church.

The funeral director lifted the casket out of the minivan. As we had planned for months, he placed it in Mark's arms.

"Are you okay? Is it heavy?" I asked.

"I can do it," Mark said, looking straight ahead.

"Are you sure?" I asked.

"I can do it."

As we approached the entrance, Mark caught sight of one of my relatives taking a last drag on a cigarette in the parking lot. Mark credits that incongruous sight with giving him a slight distraction that allowed him to muster the last bit of strength he needed to carry his son's body into the church and up the aisle.

We stepped into the church and paused for a moment as Father Baer prepared to lead the procession. I looked high above the altar at the organ pipes and the circular window framing green leaves fluttering outside. I remembered standing in that same spot six years earlier, preparing to walk up the aisle in my wedding dress.

This is really important, I thought. *Try to remember everything.*

The pianist began and we processed side by side up the aisle, Gabriel's casket in Mark's arms, my left hand on Mark's back, and Gabriel's angel blanket draped over my right arm. Mark walked tall and purposefully, being a good dad to Gabriel even then.

One of our friends said later that it was only when he saw Mark carrying the casket that it truly hit him what we had lost.

At the front of the church, Mark carefully set the casket on an adult-sized stand. I unfolded the angel blanket and helped Elena and Maria drape it over the casket.

Everyone in the church held Gabriel's footprints, photocopied on the funeral program. This message from us was printed inside: "Thank you for sharing our sorrow and helping celebrate the gift of Gabriel's short but beautiful life. The overwhelming love, prayers, and support of family and friends sustained us as we prepared for Gabriel's birth and will continue to sustain us during the journey ahead."

The music was powerful, Joe's piano playing lilting and expressive, Cathy's voice rich and strong.

Father Baer spoke of the uncertainty of life and of the apparent unfairness of a baby's life cut short. He said later that looking out onto that sea of sad faces, he was deeply aware that he needed to speak with great care, because he was holding people's hearts in his hands.

He spoke directly to Elena and Maria, asking in an exaggerated voice, "*Who* drew that *beautiful* picture on the cover of the program?" Elena was shyly but enormously pleased. He told them that they could think of Gabriel as their hero and as someone they could ask for help. And he told them that while people probably would talk about Gabriel being an angel, he really wasn't. He was something even better. He was a child of God.

To the adults, he spoke of St. Augustine's conception of God, which was that God was not the wizened, white-haired old man of many an imagination.

Augustine believed that God-ness was childlike, joyful, exuberant, creative, innocent, free. I had never heard this before. It was vastly comforting to think of Gabriel being swept joyfully into the presence of this kind of Presence.

"God," Father Baer finished, "is the youngest of all."

❧

As a meditation, Joe played a solo piano arrangement of Maurice Duruflé's "Ubi caritas," arranged by another friend and first played at our wedding. *Ubi caritas et amor, Deus ibi est.* Latin for "Where there is charity and love, there is God."

Leading the congregation in another song, Cathy was poised and brave and clear.

> Hold us with mercy, O Lord.
> Sorrow has spoken, has broken our hearts.
> Clothe us in Your care, be the life we bear. . . .
> Send us Your Spirit, O Lord.[1]

After the final note, she turned her head from the microphone, but not quite soon enough. Her sob echoed throughout the church and echoes in my memory still.

❧

At the cemetery, sitting in the front seat of the car between my parents like a little girl, I turned to look at the long line of cars with their headlights on waiting to drive in for Gabriel's burial. All those wonderful people.

The sky was threatening rain, the wind rippling the girls' dresses. The cemetery was new, with only a few dozen graves. It was located in somebody's flat old farm field, surrounded by acres of clover.

After the graveside prayers, Father Baer handed me a small silver container for sprinkling holy water on the casket. We gave it to Elena, telling her that because she was Gabriel's biggest sister she could do it first. We helped her and then Maria, took our turns, and passed it along to others.

As people started to drift away, Mark, holding Maria with one arm, stepped closer to the casket. He reached out and touched the polished lid one last time, a final benediction from father to son.

In the movies, this is the point at which the bereaved parents collapse to their knees in grief. I have never felt such emptiness and I never, ever, want to feel that again. But I also felt a sense of completion.

My job was done.

And we walked away.

epilogue

AT FIRST WE FELT PROFOUNDLY cheated that Gabriel did not live long enough to come home with us. We had come to terms with the fact that we were not going to be able to keep him very long. We weren't even praying for a miracle. Why couldn't we at least have had him for a few precious days?

This eventually dissolved into a sense of relief and gratitude. We now think of Gabriel's leaving so soon as one of his many gifts to us.

He was so sick that he would have been a terrible candidate for surgery. He would not have survived anyway. So after all those months of researching and agonizing and lying awake in the middle of the night, we had proof that we had chosen the right path for him. We ached to have him in our arms longer, but the very briefness of his visit released us forever from second thoughts about whether we should have operated or whether he might have beaten the disheartening medical odds.

Maybe the circumstances of his birth and death were our miracle. We could not have choreographed it any better. Gabriel spent his entire life literally surrounded by people who loved him. He died peacefully and painlessly in his parents' arms. If he had to leave us, it was a beautiful way to go.

❧

A day or so after Gabriel's funeral, the girls were swinging on the swing set and playing in the backyard. I was wandering aimlessly along the path of paving stones in the yard, feeling terribly heavy and terribly empty at the same time.

"Mommy, look at the butterfly," Elena said.

Oh, a butterfly. Isn't that nice.

I was not interested.

She insisted. So I wearily stepped closer and saw the strangest butterfly I have ever seen, resting on the ivy. It was asymmetrically colored, the left half strikingly different from the right. One side had the coloring of a normal monarch, mostly orange with black accents, while the other half seemed almost entirely black.

In a rush it flew right toward me and landed on the center of my chest. Just as quickly it was off again, flying around the side of the house and out of my view. Stunned and covered with goosebumps on that steamy August day, I had two instantaneous thoughts, the kind you have to struggle to translate into words. That butterfly somehow represented Gabriel, sending a message to me. And its delicate flight was like that of a satellite that dips just close enough to the gravitational pull of a star to gather power to fling itself even further into the universe.

Could the flight of that butterfly help explain Gabriel's life? Did he gather energy from his brief visit here?

Not until later did it occur to me that the butterfly's asymmetrical left and right sides might somehow symbolize Gabriel's heart. Only then did I realize that the butterfly had landed directly over my own.

❧

I always thought butterflies were used as a sort of saccharine greeting-card sentiment about death.

I would have infinitely preferred that Gabriel stay in his cocoon on earth with the rest of us, thank you very much.

I didn't learn until more than a year later that many people report (or keep to themselves for fear of being thought crazy) unusual experiences with butterflies following the death of a loved one. The Compassionate Friends group uses a butterfly as its symbol, featuring one on the cover of its magazines. Other people report unusual coincidences involving eagles or even red cardinals.

Maybe they're not coincidences.

☙

People continued to shower us with touching, meaningful gifts. On the day of the funeral, my sister Karen gave us a delicate white porcelain guardian angel, its robes and long hair flowing, cradling in its arms a baby boy. (Karen's seven-year-old son, Joseph, spotted the angel first in a store and led her to it with tears in his eyes.) Stacy and Bob, Gabriel's godparents, gave us a tiny gold baby ring. Some former neighbors gave us a heavy flat garden stone engraved with Gabriel's name and his birth date. Other friends gave us another gift for the garden, a small stone little-boy cherub. (We put both the stone and the cherub next to our roses.) We were grateful for the practical gifts too: homemade meals, gift certificates for dinner, engraved picture frames, offers to watch the girls. We were overwhelmed by the number of people—including some we didn't know—who sent cards and wrote heartfelt notes.

One of my cousins gave me a candle in a heart-shaped holder, with a note saying that I should light it whenever I was especially sad about Gabriel. She wrote that a friend had given her a candle too after one of her miscarriages. I would light that candle sometimes after the girls had gone to bed, while I was writing in Gabriel's baby book or in my journal.

At the time, Maria was in a stage in which she claimed everything smelled like strawberries. No matter what it was, she would sniff it and declare that it smelled like strawberries. One day she wanted to smell the unlit candle. I don't think she knew that the candle was anything special. She breathed in the fragrance and said,

"It smells like angels."

❧

Our insurance agent called out of the blue. *Great,* Mark thought. *We forgot to pay a premium on top of everything else.* But it wasn't about insurance.

"Your wife has been talking to my wife," the agent said. His wife was Robin, whom I knew only by first name, the woman who had offered me support throughout my pregnancy in honor of her two children who had died of HLHS. He told Mark that he was sitting in his office, looking at Gabriel's obituary in the newspaper, and crying, remembering his own daughter and son.

They had a good conversation, father to father. He cautioned Mark to brace himself for people who would ask only about how I was doing, ignoring his grief.

He also said that the grieving process would take at least a year but that people only give the father about a month. He was speaking from sad experience.

～

We had announcements printed on the cards I had spotted in a catalog soon after Gabriel's diagnosis, the cards with the watercolor of a child's hand touching the hand of God. We had one of Gabriel's handprints reproduced on the inside, along with these words:

Gabriel Kuebelbeck Neuzil
Son of Mark and Amy
Baby brother of Elena and Maria

Born August 8, 1999, 4:42 P.M.

7 pounds, 9 ounces, 22 inches
Perfect except for his heart.

Died peacefully in our arms 7:10 P.M.,
Surrounded by people who love him.

He knew only love.

It felt therapeutic to address all those envelopes and write thank-you notes to people who had helped us. Every envelope that went into the mail meant that somebody would think of Gabriel again or learn of him for the first time.

Months later, Father Baer invited us to dinner at the home of his friends Karen and Austen. It was an enjoyable evening and we had a lot to talk about, especially because the couple had lost a baby boy midway through pregnancy a few years before. As the evening went on, we also talked about Karen's career as a professional illustrator of children's books. She mentioned that one of the freelance jobs she had had before losing her own son was illustrating announcement cards for babies who had died.

You mean . . . ? Yes, she was the one who had painted that beautiful watercolor of a child's hand reaching for the hand of God, the one we so closely associate with Gabriel.

Father Baer swears he didn't know.

❧

We thought it would be good for us to see the ocean. It seemed to us that seeing the vastness of the sea and sky, feeling the saltwater breezes against our skin, and maybe watching distant storm clouds gather on the horizon might somehow help us fathom the larger world and Gabriel's place in it. So a month and a half after Gabriel died, we flew with the girls to the coast of Maine. Of course we thought of Gabriel with the sight of every crashing wave and every sunset dissolving into the sea. We felt even closer to him than before, even though his little body was buried fifteen hundred miles away.

On the Sunday when Gabriel would have been seven weeks old, we were exploring the town of Brunswick and decided to go to Mass. We sat in a pew and found printed at the top of that day's church bulletin this story:

> A woman was shattered by the loss of her brother. She asked God, "Why?" And she set off to find the answer. She came upon an old man sitting on a bench weeping. "I have suffered a great loss," he said. "I am a painter and I have lost my eyesight." They went along the road together and met a man who had lost his wife to another man, and a woman who had lost her child. Together they walked along asking, "Why?"
>
> Soon they met Jesus. Seeing them, he began to cry, and said, "I am bearing the burden of a woman who has lost her brother, a painter who is blind,

a man who has lost his dearest love, and a woman whose baby died." As he spoke, the four people embraced each other. And they grasped each other's hands.

Jesus said, "My dominion is the dominion of the heart. I cannot prevent pain, I can only heal it." "How?" asked the people. "By sharing it," Jesus replied. And then he was gone. And the four? They were left standing, holding each other.[1]

Maybe people noticed those strangers in church that day, crying.

❧

No part of our story is meant to criticize the decisions of parents who pursue medical treatment for their beloved little ones. All of us had to sort through conflicting medical opinions, and all of us made our decisions with love for our babies foremost. We have all shared the same devastation at this diagnosis, whether before birth or after, and we understand all too well the desperate desire to keep one's child alive. What parents want to bury their baby? Indeed, we might have turned to surgery too if we had learned of Gabriel's heart after he was born and had to make a decision immediately, in a state of shock. We too might have pleaded with the doctors, "Do anything! Just save our baby!"

I imagine that we will always have intense interest in developments in treating hypoplastic left heart syndrome. In one case reported about two and a half years after Gabriel died, doctors believed that an experimental and extraordinarily difficult fetal surgery prevented an unborn baby from developing HLHS. (The surgery involved guiding a needle through a valve in a beating heart that was about the size of a grape, a procedure one of the doctors characterized as "science fiction.")[2] If that had been an option for us, the chance of a cure might have been worth risking the astronomical odds. Perhaps someday there will be a breakthrough that, had it existed for Gabriel, would have altered our decisions for his care. For the sake of other HLHS babies to come, and for the people who will love them, I hope there will someday be a cure.

❧

One day, Mark retreated to our sun porch alone to look at our photographs of Gabriel. The afternoon sun filtered through the translucent ivory curtains.

Looking through the photographs taken while Gabriel was dying, he tearfully stopped at a close-up of Gabriel's face. In the picture, one of my hands is cradling Gabriel's head, and Gabriel's fingers are gripping one of Mark's fingers.

Then Mark heard something. He looked up. The sound was coming from a miniature set of wind chimes that we had received as a wedding gift. We had hung the chimes on a curtain rod against a curtain when we moved in, for lack of a better place to put them. All the windows on the porch were closed, but the chimes were moving: sparkling and musical.

✑

Our circumstances with Gabriel unfortunately cast a pall over what should have been a time of excited anticipation for others in our families. Three cousins to Gabriel were born soon after Gabriel's diagnosis and shortly after he died. At Gabriel's funeral, several women were visibly pregnant, and some women brought their nursing babies. It must have been difficult for all of those parents, who perhaps felt they should censor their happiness out of respect for our grief.

How to react to other people's babies is a common dilemma for parents grieving after miscarriage or infant loss, because if they're in their childbearing years, chances are they have friends and siblings who are too. Sooner or later the parents are going to be faced with someone else's baby. Some grieving parents find it next to impossible to even be in the same room with another baby.

We tried to separate our sorrow over Gabriel from our feelings about the other new babies. The wonderful support we received from family and friends—most of all, their patient listening while we talked incessantly and repeated ourselves endlessly—gave us permission to grieve for our baby. Parents who shared our sorrow made it easier for us to share their joy.

Stacy and Bob's daughter Avery was born exactly six weeks after Gabriel. She was born at a different hospital, but it was still wrenching for us to walk into the maternity ward to visit. Hardest for me was catching sight of a weary but happy new mother walking down the hall with her husband and newborn baby. They had flowers and balloons and were on their way home. It sent my mind reeling back to that numb, lonely wheelchair ride through the hospital corridors to the exit, with nothing to hold in my lap but a paper bag containing Gabriel's footprints and the lock of his hair. I had an irrational urge to walk up to her and tap her on the shoulder and say, *Excuse me, but I just had a baby too.*

Meeting Avery wasn't nearly as difficult. She didn't look like Gabriel; she was tinier and had surprisingly red hair and looked so . . . *Avery.* Welcome to the world, my adorable goddaughter.

❦

Children should not have to learn at such a young age that sometimes babies die.

When Avery was born, Maria's first question was "Does Avery work?" Because, of course, Gabriel didn't "work."

But I think—I hope—that the lesson our girls are learning is that some babies do die, yet we can still love them and life will go on. Death is not a taboo subject in our home.

In the first months following Gabriel's death, Maria and Elena often incorporated death into their play. One afternoon all four of us were going somewhere in the car, with both girls having snacks in their car seats in the back. Maria was insisting on pretending to be dead, and Elena was insisting that Maria should *not* play dead. They went back and forth a couple of times, and Maria held her ground. "Well," Elena countered, "can I have your chips then?" (Mark and I burst out laughing.)

After Gabriel's funeral, the girls often drew pictures for Mark and me "so you won't be sad about Gabriel." They drew stick figures of me with lines all over my face—tears—and pictures of rainbows. Now, they sometimes point out things that Gabriel might have liked or would be using. Passing through the baby aisle at the grocery store, one of them might notice the jars of baby food and ask what he would have been eating and if he might have liked the strained peas or the peaches. Or they might point out a highchair at a restaurant or a diaper-changing table in a restroom or a toy and say something like, "If Gabriel was alive, he would use that, wouldn't he, Mom?" Yes, he would have, we say. He probably would have liked it.

And he would have liked his big sisters very, very much.

⌇

Not long after Gabriel died, Mark was home alone with the girls one night, reading bedtime stories to them. One story resonated with him so much and made him so sad that he could hardly finish the book.

"Daddy, don't be sad," Maria said. She repeated it, insistent. "Daddy, don't be sad."

Wiping his eyes, he asked her why not.

And Maria, who was still mixing up her *L*s and her *N*s and has never said anything like this before or since, said:

"Because Gabriel noves you."

⌇

People often ask if we're glad we knew. Yes, a thousand times yes.

Only a small fraction of HLHS cases are detected before birth. The rest often go undetected until the baby starts turning blue, having trouble breathing, or "crashing"—sometimes just days after the parents have brought home what they assumed was a healthy baby. In some cases, no prenatal ultrasound was done; in others, the exam was done with relatively basic ultrasound machines that were not sophisticated enough to view the four chambers of the heart. Perhaps in some cases, poorly trained people were pushing the buttons on the machines and didn't notice that half the heart was missing. Just because there's an ultrasound machine in a doctor's office doesn't necessarily mean that anyone there truly knows how to use it. Complicating matters, getting a good view of the heart can be especially difficult in the third trimester of pregnancy, when calcifying rib bones and the baby's head-down position obstruct the sonographer's view.

Knowing ahead of time is especially helpful for parents who would want to try surgery, although a prenatal diagnosis does not guarantee their baby's survival. Doctors must begin treating the baby as soon after birth as possible with a prostaglandin IV drip to prop open the ductus arteriosus—the circulatory bypass that normally closes during the transition to circulation outside the womb—and try to keep the baby alive for the Norwood or a transplant. Armed with a prenatal diagnosis, parents can research the treatment options and even decide to travel across the country to deliver their baby at a transplant center or at a medical center more experienced in the Norwood than their local hospital. If the condition is diagnosed before birth, doctors have the time to determine whether the baby has other problems that would make survival after surgery unlikely. In one study, prenatal diagnosis did not affect Norwood survival, but the forewarning did lead to prompter care after birth and decreased the incidence of seizures and comas in the child.[3]

For us, our three and a half months of knowing was a gift. It gave us time to research the condition and study the options without the grave urgency of having our baby already fighting for life on machines in the neonatal intensive care unit. It gave us time to grieve even before he died, a phenomenon bereavement experts call "anticipatory grief." It allowed us to receive the support of so many wonderful people.

Most of all, knowing ahead of time meant that our precious hours with Gabriel once he was born were not filled with that initial shock and grief and confusion. He never left the room where he was born; he never left my sight. If we had not known about his heart, our caregivers would surely have swept him away from me in a desperate effort to figure out what was so terribly wrong. If we had not known, I might never have held my son in my arms while he was alive.

As we wrote to our pediatric cardiologist after Gabriel died, doctors probably consider the death of an infant to be a medical failure. But in a way we view what happened as a medical success. Doctors' expertise in diagnosing the condition and their candor in advising us about the treatment options helped us give Gabriel a good, although brief, life. And a good death.

❦

People sometimes are astonished—and perhaps a little horrified—that I walked around for three and a half months carrying a baby I knew would die.

I didn't learn until well over a year after Gabriel died that we could have aborted the pregnancy at our hospital by requesting to have labor induced at any point, thus causing him to be born very prematurely and to die earlier. Our hospital offered "terminations" up to twenty-two weeks of pregnancy in cases of nonfatal conditions such as Down syndrome and at any time during the pregnancy if the baby was not expected to live. A genetic counselor we spoke to was surprised that we had not been told about this; she said it was a standard option but that sometimes caregivers took their cues from a family in deciding whether to present it. Maybe we would have needed to bring it up first.

(In one British study, 44 percent of couples who received prenatal diagnoses of HLHS decided to abort.[4] In a study conducted in the United States, 33 percent of parents who received a diagnosis before twenty-four weeks decided to abort.)[5]

In any case, now that we've been through it, I believe that aborting my pregnancy would have been disastrous on many levels.

Most important, it would have cut Gabriel's natural life short for no good reason. Gabriel was growing normally and was in no pain, and the pregnancy was physically normal for me. Carrying him to term put me at no additional risk.

Aborting the pregnancy would have meant denying ourselves the life-changing, bittersweet, exquisite experience of holding our beautiful full-term son and hearing his cries. We didn't realize until later how crucial and sustaining those memories would be. Ending the pregnancy early would have meant rejecting a gift.

It would not have been a shortcut through our grief. If anything, our grief would have been magnified. Grief is in some ways like that childhood rhyme: "Can't go over it, can't go under it, I guess I'll have to go through it." If we had just decided to "get it over with," we would have been left with only the raw pain and without the memories of our son and the time-tested rituals of grief to soften it. Perhaps some people thought we were bringing grief upon ourselves by continuing the pregnancy and later having a full funeral and burial. Especially once we decided on comfort care, which meant that Gabriel was going to die anyway, some people must have wondered what the point was in continuing the pregnancy. They might have thought that we should just get on with our lives. But for that brief time, Gabriel *was* our life. Other than caring for our girls, there was nothing more important in our lives than waiting with Gabriel, giving him the full measure of our time and attention and love.

We also felt that if we had ended the pregnancy early, we would have been contributing to the perception that the loss of an unborn baby is of little consequence. And we would still have been in shock a week or two later, when others would have been expecting us to get over it already. Instead, my growing belly was a constant reminder to others of what we were going through. Perhaps that meant that everywhere we went, death was an uninvited and unwelcome guest. But it also resulted in our receiving an extraordinary level of support, rare for parents grieving the loss of their "invisible" babies.

Some suggest that the ethics of abortion are different when the baby is not expected to live, that in those circumstances it is more like removing life support. For me, one important distinction was that pregnancy, unlike life support, is finite; nobody stays pregnant forever. I didn't want to be responsible for removing the life support prematurely. I didn't want to be responsible for choosing his date of death. It gives us great peace to know that we protected him all the way from conception through natural death.

I believe that ending our pregnancy early would have caused us real emotional harm, as well as closed us off from the extraordinary gifts that we and our families and close friends were able to experience as we all waited with Gabriel.

Yes, Gabriel was going to die. But first he was going to live.

⁓

People generously gave us money in Gabriel's memory. We decided to channel that generosity toward helping other grieving parents create memories of their babies, especially those who were not blessed with the preparation time that we had. Memories made during those precious hours with their baby can sustain parents later, while missed opportunities can haunt forever.

So we compiled gift boxes for the hospital where Gabriel was born, to be given to parents whose baby died late in pregnancy or after birth. This wasn't meant to discount earlier losses; we just wanted to direct the gifts to parents whose situations were similar to ours.

Into each sturdy paperboard box, covered with a pattern of white roses, we put a plaster-of-Paris footprint kit like the one we used for Gabriel, a disposable camera, a baby book specifically for babies who die, a copy of the booklet *When Hello Means Goodbye*,[6] and a small stuffed toy lamb. I was very deliberate in shopping for anything that had to do with the boxes. I couldn't shop for things for Gabriel, but I could be particular about what went into the boxes. In a way it felt like my chance to shop for him. Each box also held a pretty piece of sage-green floral stationery overlaid with a sheet of translucent vellum on which I wrote that the gift was given in memory of Gabriel and "in honor of all other babies whose parents' hearts have been broken."

Elena and Maria had the special job of putting a toy lamb into each box, after they first played carefully and happily with the pile of lambs.

We knew it would be difficult to return to the birth center, our first trip there in nearly a year since Gabriel's death, but we wanted to deliver the boxes ourselves. Father Baer agreed to meet us there to say a few words of blessing over them.

Annette, our wonderful perinatal-loss guide, met us in the lobby to help carry the boxes. She asked if we might like to have them blessed in a birthing room, perhaps the very room where Gabriel was born.

Another mother and baby were already in that room. How hard it was to stand in the hallway outside that closed door and know that there was a living baby inside. We took the boxes into a labor room in the high-risk maternity area instead, which for many parents is a place of great sadness and anxiety. We set a box on the bed, its sheets fresh and taut for some other mother. Then Father Baer blessed the boxes, gifts made possible by the generous spirit of our family and friends.

We wish that no other parents would ever need those boxes. But some will. At least they will leave the hospital with a few small keepsakes of their baby, something to hold in their empty arms.

❦

For a long time after Gabriel died, whenever I saw a newborn I would just stare, not really seeing that baby but seeing Gabriel in my mind, especially if the baby was sleeping. As the weeks turned into months, I would mentally calculate how old Gabriel would be and try to figure out if the babies I'd see were close to his age. It was with renewed grief that I eventually realized that we had lost not only a newborn, but also a three month old, a six month old, a one year old . . . We would see Gabriel at none of those ages.

Baby-related junk mail and free formula samples did not help. About the time the sympathy cards tapered off, the mail carrier started delivering free samples of Huggies diapers. Because Gabriel was born alive, he was issued a birth certificate, which landed us on an assortment of mass-mailing lists. Apparently those companies don't feel the need to crosscheck birth certificates with death certificates.

An acquaintance once suggested that we were luckier than someone whose son had died in his early twenties. I wanted to say, "Well, that mother should feel lucky, because she had *twenty years* that I didn't have with my son." It is a common misperception—and an exceedingly insensitive one—that the death of an infant is less tragic and less painful because the parents didn't have time to "bond" with their child.

I still calculate how old Gabriel would be, and I still watch children around that age to see what sorts of things he might have been doing now. I don't do this with jealousy, only a sort of interested wistfulness.

Once, another mother and I struck up a casual conversation in a neighborhood bookstore while her toddler and Maria looked at books. It turned out that her son was born exactly one month before Gabriel. So I mentioned to her that I had a son at around the same time who had died and that it was nice to see what other toddlers were doing at that age. The next thing I knew, she had packed up her son and had hurried off without saying a word. It was as though she feared that I was a crazed bereaved mother who intended to kidnap her son as a replacement, like the plot of some clichéd made-for-TV movie. Whatever her reaction actually meant, I suppose she would have had no way of knowing that I didn't want anybody else's child. I only wanted Gabriel.

❧

"You are so strong." "You are taking this so well." "I could never handle losing a child—I don't know how you do it." These apparent compliments, given by well-meaning people to parents whose baby has died, are not particularly welcome. Perhaps the most puzzling platitude is "God never gives you more than you can handle." What's that supposed to mean? That weak parents get to keep their babies and strong ones don't? If that's the deal, I wish somebody had told me that going in.

The thing is, we had no choice about the fact that Gabriel had a sick heart. He died, and we still live.

◈

We found that it helped to continue to formally remember Gabriel, even if it sometimes brought tears we thought had already been shed.

Shortly after Gabriel died, we attended a non-denominational memorial service held by the Pregnancy and Infant Loss Center. In the most moving part of the ceremony, the babies' names were read aloud, and the families were invited to walk to the front of the chapel to receive a white rose in their baby's memory.

We also decided to have Gabriel's name engraved on a new memorial at a local cemetery to honor babies who have died. The Children's Memorial and Healing Garden, installed the spring after Gabriel died, features a granite wall engraved with babies' names that overlooks a pond and flower gardens. Some parents, grateful at last for the chance to formally commemorate their child's life, had their baby's name engraved even though their baby died decades ago. We just liked the idea of Gabriel's name being recorded permanently in one more place, this one close to our home, and of his name being surrounded by those of other children.

We are also grateful for the many people who are willing to say Gabriel's name in normal conversation every once in a while. He will always be part of our family, and we don't waste energy pretending otherwise.

❧

Gabriel's funeral had been beautiful. So many people, including people of other faith traditions or none at all, said later that they walked out of that church feeling truly comforted.

Even so, in the weeks afterward I was irrationally obsessed with one detail. For one part of the service, I had asked Joe to improvise on the theme of Brahms's "Lullaby," but I didn't want the improvisation to be too recognizable because I didn't want it to be maudlin. He did exactly what I had asked, beautifully. I could hear the theme while he played it during the funeral, but only because I knew what to listen for.

Afterward, I was consumed with regret. Why didn't I just go ahead and give Gabriel a lullaby? I saw it over and over in my mind: a lone oboist, walking silently to the sanctuary, lifting the instrument to her mouth, taking a slow deep breath, and filling the church with the instrument's plaintive and sorrowful sound: *Lullaby and good night, go to sleep now, my baby.* So what if it would have been maudlin. So what if everybody in the church would have ended up sobbing. He didn't even have a lullaby.

On the one-month anniversary of his death, some friends watched the girls so I could spend some much needed time alone. One of the things I did that day was sit at the piano and arrange a simple version of Brahms's "Lullaby," playing it over and over.

I like to think that Gabriel heard it.

❦

"How many children do you have?"

Such an ordinary pleasantry. Parents who have lost a child learn to make quick assessments: Do I want this person to know? If I say the true number, will I need to explain? Will the truth torpedo this conversation?

Psst, stay away from that lady, or else she might tell you about her dead baby.

Sometimes I resort to saying simply that our girls are six and four, or however old they are, rather than saying how many I have. Mark sometimes just says we have two at home. At least those answers don't make us feel that we have betrayed the memory of our son.

The girls take swimming lessons during the summer at the nearby College of St. Catherine. Parents and other children watch from the bleachers above the pool, striking up conversations among themselves to pass the time.

One day, a woman named Barb was gracefully drawing strangers into a group conversation, introducing people to one another and asking sincere questions. She mentioned that she had six children, and she was wearing a "WWJD" bracelet. She seemed like a good soul, and I decided that if The Question came up I would tell her.

At the next lesson, someone did ask me if I had more children in addition to Elena in the pool and Maria sitting next to me on the bleachers. I said yes, we also had a baby boy who had died of a fatal heart problem.

Tears welled up in Barb's eyes.

"I take care of those children," she said.

She said she was a pediatric nurse and that she cared for many heart babies. I told her that my son had hypoplastic left heart syndrome and that he lived for two and a half hours.

"Thank God he didn't live," she said, startling even me. "*Thank God.* Do you know how much those babies suffer?"

I said that we had never seen the medical after-math ourselves but that we had learned enough to choose comfort care for him.

"Good for you," she said emphatically. "You didn't torture your baby."

As the two of us talked, she said she believed aggressive medical intervention was appropriate for many babies with incurable conditions. Suffering was a part of life, she said. But she said HLHS was different.

She asked what his name was. "His name is Gabriel," I said.

"This is really weird," she said. "I had a dream last night about a little boy named Gabriel."

I asked if she knew anyone named Gabriel.

No.

She said she rarely remembered her dreams, but this one had stuck with her. For some reason, in her dream, it had been very important that she know this little boy's name. He told her several times until finally she understood and said, "Oh, you mean like the angel."

Then the dream was over.

I sat on the bleachers, wiping tears from my eyes, together with this compassionate stranger whose path dipped into mine and who left me with a luminous message: We did the right thing. And Gabriel still *is*.

෴

For many parents who have lost a baby, what would have been their child's first birthday is the worst of the anniversary dates. We felt anxious as the day approached. Sometimes just the smell of dewy summer mornings would send our minds reeling back to the days of waiting for Gabriel's birth.

Instead of dreading his birthday, we decided to try to honor it and embrace it.

On the Sunday before Gabriel's birthday, a beautiful Sunday not unlike the day he was born, much of our family gathered in our living room for an informal Mass celebrated by Father Baer. He told us that while many people think a year is plenty of time to recover after a death, no one should ever be expected to "get over it." You don't get over the fact that someone died any more than you get over the fact that you love that person. Instead, eventually, you are able to hold both truths in your heart. There were tears but also much laughter, plentiful food, and birthday balloons for all the children.

And I played one piece on the piano: Gabriel's lullaby.

On his birthday, the girls and I made a dark chocolate cake from scratch and frosted it with baby blue icing. In white icing we wrote his name and a number one. Maybe having a birthday cake for a baby who has died seems bizarre, or even morbid. But we've found that many parents celebrate what would have been their child's birthday. We weren't celebrating another year of life, but we were celebrating the fact that he had lived, if only for a short while.

We also took the girls to spend part of the day at the Minneapolis Planetarium. Some friends had adopted a star in Gabriel's name, a fantastically thoughtful gift. So we were given a brief private showing of "Gabriel's star" among the stars twinkling and blinking in the black eternity.

Happy birthday, sweetheart.

~

You might think that having your child die in your arms would be the stuff of endless nightmares. It wasn't. Again, I believe that was because of the gift of knowing ahead of time. We had time to prepare to make the most of every moment he did live. We had time to prepare ourselves and confront our fears. And the advance knowledge made it possible for us to allow Gabriel to have a natural, painless, peaceful death. I was more afraid that he would die in a stranger's arms—or connected to a myriad of tubes, alone—than of him dying in my own.

In the first weeks after his death, I would sometimes try to conjure him up during those fleeting moments of lucid dreaming just before waking up.

I would call his name through the mist. I never was able to will him to appear.

Around the time of Gabriel's first birthday, I had only my second dream about him, as strikingly vivid as the one I had right after he died. Mark and I and Elena and Maria were all sitting together on a bed in a sun-drenched room somewhere, playing and laughing, when suddenly I was aware of a small boy standing patiently on the floor at the foot of the bed. He looked about a year old. I had the impression that he didn't yet know how to walk.

Gabriel, is that you? I said. I already knew that it was. He had curly blond hair, a little-boy version of our girls' faces, and beautiful blue eyes. He held out his arms so I could lift him onto the bed, where he sat happily in my lap, giggling and babbling and watching his sisters play. He let me hold him for what seemed like the longest time, much longer than a wriggly one year old would normally sit still. Again and again I kissed his forehead, sweet and warm.

Finally we somehow knew that it was time for him to "go back." Mark helped get him ready and took him outside into the sunshine, where a black car and some people were waiting.

And it was okay.

I awoke with tears in my eyes and with a sensation of his weight in my arms. And with a feeling of peace.

So goodbye for now, our beautiful baby.

We are waiting to hold you again.

acknowledgments

IF I WERE TO THANK PROPERLY all the people who helped us on our journey with Gabriel and, later, who helped midwife this book, it would be too heavy to lift. To all of you, please consider this book my expression of heartfelt gratitude.

As is probably clear from the preceding pages, the support we received while we waited with Gabriel was extraordinary. Continuing a pregnancy when the baby is expected to die is not easy for anyone involved. With no guide other than their own hearts, family and friends rallied to support us and to honor Gabriel's life. As we discovered together, the journey was bittersweet, painful, joyful, unforgettable, and blessed. This story is their story too. It is my hope that as prenatal testing continues to advance, resulting inevitably in more parents receiving devastating diagnoses before birth, those parents may be similarly blessed.

Deepest thanks go to our families, especially our parents, Jim and Carol Kuebelbeck and Jack and Fran Neuzil. Gabriel is blessed to have you as grandparents, aunts, uncles, and cousins. To our dear friends Barbara and Gene McGivern: I believe Gabriel thinks of you as Aunt Barb and Uncle Gene. Others who were of special help include Father Bill Baer and Annette Klein, R.N., perinatal-loss educator and mother of Courtney. Parents who helped light our path include Tom and Jean Levandowski, parents of Claire; Fran Cava, mother of Alexander; Kim Hazlett, mother of Daniel; Steve Laumakis and Mary Thomas, parents of Steven; and Mary Comford, mother of Maureen. Thank you to the staff and volunteers at the former Pregnancy and Infant Loss Center, especially Charlene Nelson, mother of David, and Robin and Dave Abraham, parents of Corinne and John. Thanks to photographer Claudia Danielson, who so compassionately captured the poignancy of this pregnancy on film. Thank you to Tim Nelson of A Place to Remember, father of Kathleen, for helping us announce Gabriel's birth, and to artist Karen Ritz Rockcastle, mother of William, whose lovely watercolor helped me visualize Gabriel placing his little hand into the hand of God. Joe and Cathy

Kalkman comforted us with music, and Gayla Lindt and Eric Amel both literally and figuratively gave us their creative light. Thank you to Cheryl and Dave Wittman, parents of Olivia, and Char and Jeff Kandt, parents of Aaron, and all the other parents who are continuing the idea of "Gabriel's boxes" in memory of their own sweet babies.

To my literary agent, Brian DeFiore, thank you, thank you for believing in this project. Thank you to the many good people at Loyola Press, especially editorial director Jim Manney, my thoughtful editor, Heidi Hill, and designer Eva Vincze. Cathi Lammert, R.N., executive director of SHARE Pregnancy and Infant Loss Support and mother of Christopher, helped me put practices regarding infant death into historical context. Thanks to Todd Orjala for his encouragement in writing this book. A number of people read drafts of the manuscript and made insightful suggestions; those readers include pediatric cardiologist Lee Pyles, M.D., Annette Klein, Father Baer, Dave Nimmer, and Mary McCaslin Thompson.

To my husband, Mark Neuzil, I can't imagine walking this path without you. Thank you for the three best gifts I've ever received: Elena, Maria, and Gabriel.

Amy Kuebelbeck
June 2002

endnotes

Chapter 1

1. Elisabeth Kübler-Ross, *On Death and Dying* (New York: Macmillan, 1969).

Chapter 2

1. "Congenital Heart Defects in Children Fact Sheet," American Heart Association, http://www. americanheart.org.

2. S. LeRoy, R.N., M.S.N., L. Callow, R.N., M.S.N., C.P.N.P., and K. George, R.N., M.S.N., C.P.N.P., "Hypoplastic Left Heart Syndrome," University of Michigan Congenital Heart Center for Parents, http://www-umchc.pdc.med.umich.edu/parents/ d-hypoplastic.html.

3. M. Samanek, "Boy:Girl Ratio in Children Born with Different Forms of Cardiac Malformation: A Population-Based Study," *Pediatric Cardiology* 15, no. 2 (March–April 1994): 53–57.

4. Marshall L. Jacobs and William I. Norwood, "Hypoplastic Left Heart Syndrome," in *Glenn's Thoracic and Cardiovascular Surgery,* 6th ed., ed. Arthur E. Baue (Stamford, Conn.: Appleton and Lange, 1996), 1271.

5. Carl Backer, Edward L. Bove, Vincent R. Zales, et al., "Hypoplastic Left Heart Syndrome," in *Pediatric Cardiac Surgery,* 2nd ed., ed. Constantine Mavroudis (St. Louis: Mosby, 1994), 442.

6. S. LeRoy, et al., "Hypoplastic Left Heart Syndrome," http://www-umchc.pdc.med.umich.edu/parents/ d-hypo-norw.html.

7. Jacobs and Norwood, 1271.

8. S. LeRoy, et al., "Hypoplastic Left Heart Syndrome," http://www-umchc.pdc.med.umich.edu/parents/ d-hypo-hemi.html.

9. Ibid., http://www-umchc.pdc.med.umich.edu/ parents/d-hypo-font.html.

10. The Pediatric Cardiac Care Consortium, based at the University of Minnesota, is a registry for data from forty-three participating medical centers where the Norwood is performed. In 2000, the most recent year for which statistics were available from the consortium,

46 percent of infants survived the first stage. Statistic verified by Christine Hills, consortium program coordinator.

11. E. L. Bove, "Current Status of Staged Reconstruction for Hypoplastic Left Heart Syndrome," *Pediatric Cardiology* 19, no. 4 (July–August 1998): 308–15.

12. William T. Mahle, Thomas L. Spray, Gil Wernovsky, et al., "Survival after Reconstructive Surgery for Hypoplastic Left Heart Syndrome: A 15-Year Experience from a Single Institution," *Circulation* 102, supplement 3 (7 November 2000): 136–41.

13. Warren King, "Learning Major Surgery on Tiny Hearts," *Seattle Times,* 31 March 1997.

14. S. LeRoy, et al., "Hypoplastic Left Heart Syndrome," http://www-umchc.pdc.med.umich.edu/parents/ d-hypo-norw.html.

15. "Cadaveric Donor Characteristics, 1991 to 2000: Heart Donors," 2001 Annual Report of the U.S. Organ Procurement and Transplantation Network and the Scientific Registry for Transplant Recipients: Transplant Data 1991–2000. Department of Health and Human Services, Health Resources and Services Administration, Office of Special Programs, Division of Transplantation, Rockville, MD; United Network for Organ Sharing, Richmond, VA; University Renal Research and Education Association, Ann Arbor, MI. Retrieved 1 May 2002 from http://ustransplant.org/ annual.html.

16. Richard A. Schaefer, "Perspective on Neonatal Heart Transplantation," from *Legacy: Daring to Care,* rev. ed. (Loma Linda, Calif.: Loma Linda University and Medical Center), http://www.llu.edu/info/legacy/ Legacy4.html.

17. L. L. Bailey, S. L. Nehlsen-Cannarella, W. Concepcion, et al., "Baboon-to-Human Cardiac Xenotransplantation in a Neonate," *Journal of the American Medical Association* 254, no. 23 (20 December 1985): 3321–29.

18. Robert Steinbrook, "Rare Infant-to-Infant Heart Transplant Done," *Los Angeles Times,* 22 November 1985.

19. "Patient Survival and Standard Errors at 3 Months, 1 Year, 3 Years and 5 Years: Heart Transplants," 2001 OPTN/SRTR Annual Report 1991–2000. HHS/HRSA/OSP/DOT; UNOS; URREA. http:// ustransplant.org/annual.html.

20. S. LeRoy, et al., "Hypoplastic Left Heart Syndrome," http://www-umchc.pdc.med.umich.edu/parents/ d-hypoplastic.html.

21. "Newborn Receives a New Heart 90 Minutes into Life," Associated Press, published in the *Minneapolis Star Tribune,* 15 November 1996. The AP transmitted a follow-up story when the baby died, but not all newspapers that printed the first story also printed the news of the baby's death.

22. Deborah L. Davis, *Loving and Letting Go: For Parents Who Decided to Turn Away from Aggressive Medical Intervention for Their Critically Ill Newborns* (Omaha, Nebr.: Centering Corporation, 1993), 14.

23. Office of the Revisor of Statutes, State of Minnesota, Minnesota Statutes 2001, secs. 145.411 (http://www .revisor.leg.state.mn.us/stats/145/411.html) and 145.412 (http://www.revisor.leg.state.mn.us/ stats/145/412.html).

24. Letter from P. John Seward, M.D., executive vice president, American Medical Association, to U.S. Sen. Rick Santorum (19 May 1997), as cited in *Born-Alive Infants Protection Act of 2001*, Constitution Subcommittee of the House Committee on the Judiciary, 107th Cong., 1st sess., 2001, H. Rept. 107–186, http://www.house.gov/judiciary/ 107-186.pdf.

Chapter 3

1. A Place to Remember, 1885 University Ave., Suite 110, St. Paul, MN 55104, http://www .aplacetoremember.com.

2. Cathi Lammert, R.N., executive director of SHARE Pregnancy and Infant Loss Support, interview by author, 23 May 2002.

3. Mae M. Bookmiller, R.N., and George Loveridge Bowen, A.B., M.D., *Textbook of Obstetrics and Obstetric Nursing* (Philadelphia: W. B. Saunders Company, 1956), 663.

4. Larry G. Peppers and Ronald J. Knapp, *Motherhood and Mourning: Perinatal Death* (New York: Praeger Publishing, 1980), 105.

5. Lammert, interview.

6. *Some Babies Die: An Exploration of Stillbirth and Neonatal Death,* dir. Martyn Langdon Down, nar. Dr. Elisabeth Kübler-Ross, 55 min., University of California Extension Media, 1986, videocassette.

7. *A Most Important Picture: A Very Tender Manual for Taking Pictures of Stillborn Babies and Infants Who Die* (Omaha, Nebr.: Centering Corporation, 1997), 2. See also James Van Der Zee, Owen Dodson, and Camille Billops, *The Harlem Book of the Dead* (Dobbs Ferry, N.Y.: Morgan and Morgan, 1978).

8. Jessica Mitford, *The American Way of Birth* (New York: Dutton, 1992), 30.

9. Ibid., 47.

10. T. J. Matthews, M.S., Marian F. MacDorman, Ph.D., and Fay Menacker, Dr.P.H., Division of Vital Statistics, "Infant Mortality Statistics from the 1999 Period Linked Birth/Infant Death Data Set," *National Vital Statistics Reports* 50, no. 4 (30 January 2002). National Center for Health Statistics, http://www.cdc .gov/nchs/data/nvsr/nvsr50/nvsr50_04.pdf.

11. Stephanie J. Ventura, M.A., William D. Mosher, Ph.D., Sally C. Curtin, M.A., Joyce C. Abma, Ph.D.,

Division of Vital Statistics; and Stanley Henshaw,
Ph.D., The Alan Guttmacher Institute, "Highlights
of Trends in Pregnancies and Pregnancy Rates by
Outcome: Estimates for the United States, 1976–96,"
National Vital Statistics Reports 47, no. 29 (15 December
1999). National Center for Health Statistics, http://
www.cdc.gov/nchs/data/nvsr/nvsr47/
nvs47_29.pdf.

12. "Fetal Death Detail Record, 1998," CDC Wonder,
http://wonder.cdc.gov/wonder/sci_data/mort/fetldeth/
type_txt/ftldth98.asp.

13. Margaret Mead and Rhoda Metraux, "A Way of Seeing"
(1970), in *The New Beacon Book of Quotations by Women,*
comp. Rosalie Maggio (Boston: Beacon Press, 1996),
466.

14. Andrew Greeley and Mary Greeley Durkin, *How to Save
the Catholic Church* (New York: Viking, 1984), 33.

Chapter 4
1. Archbishop Harry J. Flynn, "Gabriel Was Strong
Testimony to Life," *The Catholic Spirit,* 9 September 1999.

Chapter 5
1. "Send Us Your Spirit," © 1985, Daniel L. Schutte and
New Dawn Music, 5536 N.E. Hassalo, Portland, OR
97213. All rights reserved. Used with permission.

Epilogue
1. "Holding Each Other," from William J. Bausch,
A World of Stories for Preachers and Teachers: And All

Who Love Stories That Move and Challenge (Mystic, Conn.: Twenty-Third Publications, 1998), 274–75, as paraphrased in the Saint John the Baptist Parish Community bulletin, 26 September 1999.

2. Denise Grady, "Operation on Fetus's Heart Valve Called a 'Science Fiction' Success," *New York Times*, 25 February 2002, sec. A.

3. W. T. Mahle, R. R. Clancy, S. P. McGaurn, et al., "Impact of Prenatal Diagnosis on Survival and Early Neurologic Morbidity in Neonates with the Hypoplastic Left Heart Syndrome," *Pediatrics* 107, no. 6 (June 2001): 1277–82.

4. K. J. Brackley, M. D. Kilby, J. G. Wright, et al., "Outcome after Prenatal Diagnosis of Hypoplastic Left Heart Syndrome," *The Lancet* 356, no. 9236 (30 September 2000): 1143–47.

5. L. D. Allen, H. D. Apfel, and B. F. Printz, "Outcome after Prenatal Diagnosis of the Hypoplastic Left Heart Syndrome," *Heart* 79, no. 4 (April 1998): 371–73.

6. Pat Schwiebert and Paul Kirk, *When Hello Means Goodbye* (Portland, Ore.: Perinatal Loss, 1998).

Advance praise for *Waiting with Gabriel* . . .

"Kuebelbeck writes about the unthinkable and does it with beauty, grace, and a profound understanding of the true meaning of death as it relates to the living. This book makes us think about the difficult questions of medical ethics and intervention—but ultimately, it is a mother's goodbye kiss, and as such, it is heartbreaking, life affirming, and wise."
> —RICHARD PAUL EVANS, author of *The Christmas Box* and *The Last Promise*

"Amy Kuebelbeck's touching story of her son's short life will bring solace to all. Her gentle words and shared personal experience will provide an inner strength and positive guidance to those who make the decision of comfort care for their baby."
> —CATHI LAMMERT, R.N., executive director of SHARE Pregnancy and Infant Loss Support, Inc.

"With candor and tenderness, Amy Kuebelbeck offers companionship to those of us who face the bitter reality of loving and losing a child. From the awkward questions of strangers and the unforgettable compassion of caregivers to the countercultural courage of broken-hearted parents, *Waiting with Gabriel* gives readers a glimpse into a sacred season in which a family savors life in the face of death."
> —NANCY GUTHRIE, author of *Holding On to Hope*

"After the tears, readers of *Waiting with Gabriel* will come to understand and embrace the ephemeral yet indestructible bond between mother and father and child. In an era of advancing medical technologies, there will inevitably be failures and setbacks. *Waiting with Gabriel* teaches parents and medical professionals alike to confront these failures with love and hope and compassion."
  —MICHAEL BERMAN, M.D., clinical professor of obstetrics and gynecology, Yale University School of Medicine

"Exquisite and tender, . . . *Waiting with Gabriel* is a love story that inspires us to live wisely and see the treasures in adversity. If you are going through a similar ordeal, this book will walk with you, illuminating your path and comforting you with the realization that you are not alone."
  —DEBORAH L. DAVIS, PH.D., author of *Empty Cradle, Broken Heart* and *Loving and Letting Go*

"*Waiting with Gabriel* is a beautiful story, not about death and grief but about being fully present through every precious moment of life and loss. Amy Kuebelbeck reminds us of how important it is to embrace our feelings and give them ritual expression—to love well, grieve well, and remember well."
  —SARAH YORK, author of *Remembering Well* and *The Holy Intimacy of Strangers*

"A deeply personal and beautifully written book that will break your heart wide open. Amy Kuebelbeck's story teaches us about grieving and healing, living and loving. Gabriel's brief life is truly a gift to us all."
  —DENISE ROY, author of *My Monastery Is a Minivan*

waiting with Gabriel